RAMADAN
LESSONS
FROM THE NOBLE QURAN
AND AUTHENTIC SUNNAH

VOLUME ONE: 1439 (2018)
PREPARED BY: MOOSAA RICHARDSON

First Print Edition: Sha'baan 1439 (May 2018)

Revised Second Edition: Sha'baan 1440 (April 2019)

Richardson, Moosaa.

Ramadhaan Lessons From the Noble Quran and Authentic Sunnah / Author: Moosaa Richardson.

ISBN 978-1717535283

1. Nonfiction —Religion —Islam —Koran & Sacred Writings.

2. Education & Reference —Study Aids —General.

TABLE OF CONTENTS

INTRODUCTION

All praise is due to Allah, the Lord, Creator, and Sustainer of all things. May He raise the rank of and grant peace to the final seal of all of His Prophets and Messengers, Muhammad, and all of his respected family and noble companions.

As we enter Ramadhaan, the month of fasting, the month of the Quran, the month of *taqwa* (piety), we beg our Gracious Lord that He bestow upon us understanding of His Magnificent Book, the Quran.

The 30 lessons of this book were designed specifically as a primary study tool for our daily classes in Ramadhaan 1439 (2018) at the First Muslim Mosque in Pittsburgh, Pennsylvania (USA). Each lesson consists of:

1. A Quranic passage
2. Some or all of the vocabulary from the passage
3. An Arabic Language benefit
4. Tafseer benefits
5. A hadeeth related to the topic of the Quranic passage
6. Benefits of the hadeeth
7. An extension activity (research, memorization, or action plans)

The first five lessons of the book focus on the five Verses about fasting in *Soorah al-Baqarah*. Then, the Quranic passages were selected to represent and balanced study of a variety of important topics in Creed, Methodology, Fiqh, and Manners.

Those who have not yet committed themselves to serious study of the Arabic Language may not be able to follow the Arabic module of each lesson. Do not get discouraged, but instead allow these brief modules to be daily reminders about the importance of studying the language of the Quran. We have a Book of revelation from our Lord, preserved in the language it was revealed in, for over 1,400 years. It contains guidance, legislation, and information about the purpose of life and what happens after we die! It clarifies the Truth regarding the matters that the people around us differ over. So, of course, we recognize the importance of learning Arabic, and we ask Allah for success!

This workbook has not been designed for independent self-study. To maximize your benefit from these lessons, download or listen to the freely available recordings of the classes and follow along using this workbook. Here is how you can access our high-quality MP3 recordings:

Go to **www.Spreaker.com/radio1mm** and click on the **"SHOWS"** menu, as illustrated below:

The "shows" are in alphabetical order. Scroll down to **"Ramadhaan Lessons 1439"** and click on it. You will then see a list of the complete set of recordings, *in shaa' Allah*.

I ask Allah that He grant me and you success in attaining His Pleasure and drawing near to Him. May He raise the rank of his Messenger, Muhammad, and grant him and his family and companions an abundance of peace.

ABUL-'ABBAAS MOOSAA RICHARDSON

Education Director of the First Muslim Mosque of Pittsburgh, Pennsylvania

1.1 QURAN STUDY

﴿ يَـٰٓأَيُّهَا ٱلَّذِينَ ءَامَنُوا۟ كُتِبَ عَلَيْكُمُ ٱلصِّيَامُ كَمَا كُتِبَ عَلَى ٱلَّذِينَ مِن قَبْلِكُمْ لَعَلَّكُمْ تَتَّقُونَ ﴾ البقرة: ١٨٣

"O you who have believed! Prescribed upon you is fasting, as it was prescribed upon those before you, in order for you to attain *taqwa* (fear and consciousness of Allah)." [2:183]

1.2 VOCABULARY OF THE VERSE

كُتِبَ عَلَيْكُم	كُتِبَ	الَّذِينَ آمَنُوا
تَتَّقُونَ	الَّذِينَ مِنْ قَبْلِكُمْ	الصِّيَامُ

1.3 AN ARABIC LANGUAGE BENEFIT

You can change from active voice (مَبْنِيٌّ لِلْمَعْلُوم), like كَتَبَ ("He wrote"), to passive voice (مَبْنِيٌّ لِلْمَجْهُول), like كُتِبَ ("It was written"), by changing the *harakaat* (vowelling) of the verb. Practice this with some other verbs in table below:

تَرَكَ ⇐ ترك	أَكَلَ ⇐ أُكِلَ	فَعَلَ ⇐ فُعِلَ
ضَرَبَ ⇐	رَسَمَ ⇐	دَرَسَ ⇐
غَفَرَ ⇐	خَلَقَ ⇐	جَعَلَ ⇐

1.4 TAFSEER BENEFITS

The call: "O you who believe..."	
Definition of *eemaan*	
Fasting has been prescribed	
The fasting of previous nations	
The overall goal of fasting	
Definition of *taqwa*	

1.5 HADEETH STUDY

عَنْ أَبِي هُرَيْرَةَ رَضِيَ اللهُ عَنْهُ، عَنِ النَّبِيِّ صَلَّى اللهُ عَلَيْهِ وَسَلَّمَ، قَالَ: «يَقُولُ اللهُ عَزَّ وَجَلَّ: الصَّوْمُ لِي، وَأَنَا أَجْزِي بِهِ، يَدَعُ شَهْوَتَهُ وَأَكْلَهُ وَشُرْبَهُ مِنْ أَجْلِي، وَالصَّوْمُ جُنَّةٌ، وَلِلصَّائِمِ فَرْحَتَانِ: فَرْحَةٌ حِينَ يُفْطِرُ، وَفَرْحَةٌ حِينَ يَلْقَى رَبَّهُ، وَلَخُلُوفُ فَمِ الصَّائِمِ أَطْيَبُ عِنْدَ اللهِ مِنْ رِيحِ المِسْكِ.» [مُتَّفَقٌ عَلَيْهِ]

On the authority of Aboo Hurayrah (may Allah be pleased with him), from the Prophet (may Allah raise his rank and grant him peace), who said: **"Allah, the Mighty and Majestic, has said: Fasting is for Me, and I alone provide its reward. He leaves his desires, his food and drink, for My sake! Fasting is a shield, and a fasting person shall have two occasions of joy: one when he breaks his fast, and another when he meets his Lord. Certainly, the smell of a fasting person's breath is better with Allah than the fragrance of musk."** [Agreed upon]

1.6 BENEFITS OF THE HADEETH

Aboo Hurayrah	
"*Hadeeth qudsee*"	
Sincerity in fasting	
Fasting people abstain from:	1
	2
	3
Benefits of fasting (as found in this hadeeth)	1
	2
	3
	4
	5
The joys of obedience	
Vs. temporary "joy" of sin	
Outward appearances	

1.7 RESEARCH: How many benefits and advantages of fasting (spiritual, medical, or otherwise) can you compile?

2.1 QURAN STUDY

﴿ أَيَّامًا مَّعْدُودَاتٍ فَمَن كَانَ مِنكُم مَّرِيضًا أَوْ عَلَىٰ سَفَرٍ فَعِدَّةٌ مِّنْ أَيَّامٍ أُخَرَ وَعَلَى الَّذِينَ يُطِيقُونَهُ فِدْيَةٌ طَعَامُ مِسْكِينٍ فَمَن تَطَوَّعَ خَيْرًا فَهُوَ خَيْرٌ لَّهُ وَأَن تَصُومُواْ خَيْرٌ لَّكُمْ إِن كُنتُمْ تَعْلَمُونَ ﴾

البقرة: ١٨٤

"A set number of days, and whoever of you is ill or upon a journey, then some other days (are made up in place of the days missed). Upon those who are capable (but do not fast) is a ransom due, feeding a poor person. Whoever does more good voluntarily, that is better for him. Yet, fasting is better for you, if you only knew." [2:184]

2.2 VOCABULARY OF THE VERSE

عَلَىٰ سَفَرٍ		مَرِيضًا	أَيَّامًا مَعْدُودَاتٍ
الَّذِينَ يُطِيقُونَهُ		أَيَّامٍ أُخَرَ	عِدَّةٌ
تَطَوَّعَ		طَعَامُ مِسْكِينٍ	فِدْيَةٌ
إِنْ كُنْتُمْ تَعْلَمُونَ		وَأَنْ تَصُومُوا	خَيْرٌ

2.3 AN ARABIC LANGUAGE BENEFIT

Single nouns which end with two *dhammahs* of *tanween*, like خَيْرٌ (good), can also end with two *fat-hahs* of *tanween*, and an *alif* is written and pronounced, like خَيْرًا. Practice this with some single nouns below, and then finish filling in the table, adding three more single nouns:

مَجْرُورٍ	مَنْصُوبًا	مَرْفُوعٌ
خَيْرٍ	خَيْرًا	خَيْرٌ
		مَرِيضٌ
سَفَرٍ		
أَيَّامٍ		
		طَعَامٌ
مِسْكِينٍ		

2.4 TAFSEER BENEFITS

A number of days	
Sick people are excused	
Travelers are excused	
An abrogated option	
Some of the ruling remains	
Definition of a "*miskeen*"	

2.5 HADEETH STUDY

عَنْ جَابِرِ بْنِ عَبْدِ اللَّهِ رَضِيَ اللَّهُ عَنْهُمَا، قَالَ: كَانَ رَسُولُ اللَّهِ صَلَّى اللَّهُ عَلَيْهِ وَسَلَّمَ فِي سَفَرٍ، فَرَأَى زِحَامًا وَرَجُلًا قَدْ ظُلِّلَ عَلَيْهِ، فَقَالَ: «مَا هَذَا؟» فَقَالُوا: صَائِمٌ. فَقَالَ: «لَيْسَ مِنَ الْبِرِّ الصَّوْمُ فِي السَّفَرِ.»

[مُتَّفَقٌ عَلَيْهِ]

On the authority of Jaabir ibn 'Abdillah (may Allah be pleased with him and his father): The Messenger of Allah (may Allah raise his rank and grant him peace) was on a journey, and he saw a crowd of people around a man who passed out. **"What's this?"** he asked. They said, "Fasting." He replied, **"It is not from piety to fast during a journey."** [Agreed upon]

2.6 BENEFITS OF THE HADEETH

Jaabir ibn 'Abdillaah	
Piety is not refusing concessions	
Ease of worship in Islam	
The ruling on fasting during a journey	1 Recommended:
	2 Permissible:
	3 Disliked:
	4 Prohibited:

2.7 RESEARCH: Find this hadeeth in *Saheeh al-Bukhaaree*. What chapter did the author use for it? Consider this hadeeth and its chapter title as it relates to the chapters before it and after it, to gain some insight about and appreciate the *fiqh* of Imaam al-Bukhaaree (may Allah have Mercy on him).

3.1 QURAN STUDY

شَهْرُ رَمَضَانَ ٱلَّذِىٓ أُنزِلَ فِيهِ ٱلْقُرْءَانُ هُدًى لِّلنَّاسِ وَبَيِّنَـٰتٍ مِّنَ ٱلْهُدَىٰ وَٱلْفُرْقَانِ فَمَن شَهِدَ مِنكُمُ ٱلشَّهْرَ فَلْيَصُمْهُ وَمَن كَانَ مَرِيضًا أَوْ عَلَىٰ سَفَرٍ فَعِدَّةٌ مِّنْ أَيَّامٍ أُخَرَ يُرِيدُ ٱللَّهُ بِكُمُ ٱلْيُسْرَ وَلَا يُرِيدُ بِكُمُ ٱلْعُسْرَ وَلِتُكْمِلُوا۟ ٱلْعِدَّةَ وَلِتُكَبِّرُوا۟ ٱللَّهَ عَلَىٰ مَا هَدَىٰكُمْ وَلَعَلَّكُمْ تَشْكُرُونَ ﴿ البقرة: ١٨٥

"The month of Ramadhaan is when the Quran was sent down, guidance for Mankind and clarifications of the guidance and the Criterion. Whoever of you witnesses the month, let him fast it. Whoever is ill or on a journey, then some other days (are made up later). Allah wants ease for you, and He does not want difficulty for you, so you could complete the amount (of days of fasting), and so that you could declare the Greatness of Allah, for what He has guided you to, and in order for you to be grateful." [2:185]

3.2 VOCABULARY OF THE VERSE

هُدًى لِّلنَّاسِ	أُنْزِلَ فِيهِ الْقُرْآنُ	شَهْرُ رَمَضَانَ
فَمَنْ شَهِدَ	الْفُرْقَانِ	بَيِّنَاتٍ

15

يُرِيدُ اللهُ بِكُمْ	فَلْيَصُمْهُ	الشَّهْرَ
وَلِتُكْمِلُوا العِدَّةَ	العُسْرَ	اليُسْرَ
وَلَعَلَّكُمْ تَشْكُرُونَ	عَلَى مَا هَدَاكُمْ	وَلِتُكَبِّرُوا اللهَ

3.3 AN ARABIC LANGUAGE BENEFIT

Using opposites helps explain a matter with clarity. Think about how Allah explains that He wants ease for us, and He does not want hardship for us. While we could extract from the first phrase that Allah does not want hardship for us, He still stated it verbatim, in order to stress that meaning and clarify it. Try to put these meanings together in the table below, and complete it with one more set of opposites from yourself:

وَلَا يُرِيدُ بِكُمْ العُسْرَ ⇐	يُرِيدُ اللهُ بِكُمْ اليُسْرَ ⇐	اليُسْرَ / العُسْرَ
وَلَا _____ ⇐	يُرِيدُ اللهُ بِكُمْ _____ ⇐	الخَيْرَ / الشَّرَّ
_____ ⇐	يُرِيدُ _____ ⇐	الإِيمَانَ / ____
_____ ⇐	_____ ⇐	____ / ____

3.4 TAFSEER BENEFITS

The revelation of Quran	
Definition of Quran	
Seeing/witnessing the "month"?	
This abrogates a previous Verse	
The concession is emphasized	
The wisdom of this legislation	1
	2

	3
	4
	5

3.5 HADEETH STUDY

عَنْ أَبِي هُرَيْرَةَ رَضِيَ اللَّهُ عَنْهُ، قَالَ: قَالَ النَّبِيُّ صَلَّى اللهُ عَلَيْهِ وَسَلَّمَ: «صُومُوا لِرُؤْيَتِهِ، وَأَفْطِرُوا لِرُؤْيَتِهِ، فَإِنْ غُبِّيَ عَلَيْكُمْ فَأَكْمِلُوا عِدَّةَ شَعْبَانَ ثَلاَثِينَ.» [مُتَّفَقٌ عَلَيْهِ]

On the authority of Aboo Hurayrah (may Allah be pleased with him), the Prophet (may Allah raise his rank and grant him peace), said: "**Fast according to its sighting, and break your fast according to its sighting. If it is obscured from your view, complete the term of *Sha'baan* as 30 [days].**" [Agreed upon]

3.6 BENEFITS OF THE HADEETH

Aboo Hurayrah	
The connection to the Verse	
How the month begins and ends	
Fasting begins in three ways	1
	2
	3
Predictions and calculations	

17

3.7 RESEARCH: Can a month ever be 28 days? If so, how?

4.1 QURAN STUDY

وَإِذَا سَأَلَكَ عِبَادِى عَنِّى فَإِنِّى قَرِيبٌ أُجِيبُ دَعْوَةَ ٱلدَّاعِ إِذَا دَعَانِ فَلْيَسْتَجِيبُواْ لِى وَلْيُؤْمِنُواْ بِى لَعَلَّهُمْ يَرْشُدُونَ ﴿ البقرة: ١٨٦ ﴾

"And when My servants ask you about Me, then I am certainly near. I respond to the prayer of every supplicant whenever he calls upon Me. So let them respond to Me and believe in Me, in order for them to be rightly guided." [2:186]

4.2 VOCABULARY OF THE VERSE

وَإِذَا سَأَلَكَ	عِبَادِي عَنِّي	فَإِنِّي قَرِيبٌ
أُجِيبُ	دَعْوَةَ الدَّاعِ	إِذَا دَعَانِ
فَلْيَسْتَجِيبُوا لِي	وَلْيُؤْمِنُوا بِي	لَعَلَّهُمْ يَرْشُدُونَ

4.3 AN ARABIC LANGUAGE BENEFIT

Adding a *"laam al-amr"* to a present tense verb changes it to a command in the third person. For example, يَسْتَجِيبُونَ (they respond) becomes فَلْيَسْتَجِيبُوا (let them respond) when that *laam* is added. The case of the verb changes from *marfoo'* to *majzoom* when this *laam* is used. Look at how this operation works in the table below, and try to apply the same method to the new words and complete the table:

﴿فَلْيَسْتَجِيبُوا لِي﴾	+ف +ل ⇐	يَسْتَجِيبُونَ لِي
﴿وَلْيُؤْمِنُوا بِي﴾	+و +ل ⇐	يُؤْمِنُونَ بِي
﴿ ﴾	+ف +ل ⇐	يَصُومُهُ
﴿ ﴾	+ف +ل ⇐	يَعْبُدُونَ رَبَّ هَذَا البَيْتِ
« »	+ف +ل ⇐	يَقُولُ خَيْرًا

4.4 TAFSEER BENEFITS

People ask about Allah	
Allah is certainly near	
A great generality	
Generalities have exceptions	
Two actions are required	1
	2
Guidance is the result	
Du'aa' (supplication) is worship	
Examples of errors in *du'aa'*	1 *Shirk* (polytheism)
	2 *Bid'ah* (innovation)
	3 *Ta'addee* (transgression)

4.5 HADEETH STUDY

عَنْ أَبِي هُرَيْرَةَ رَضِيَ اللهُ عَنْهُ: أَنَّ رَسُولَ اللهِ صَلَّى اللهُ عَلَيْهِ وَسَلَّمَ قَالَ:

«أَقْرَبُ مَا يَكُونُ الْعَبْدُ مِنْ رَبِّهِ، وَهُوَ سَاجِدٌ، فَأَكْثِرُوا الدُّعَاءَ.»

[أَخْرَجَهُ مُسْلِمٌ]

On the authority of Aboo Hurayrah (may Allah be pleased with him), the Messenger of Allah (may Allah raise his rank and grant him peace) said: **"The closest a servant can become to his Lord is when he is prostrating, so make a lot of *du'aa'* [when prostrating]."** [*Sahih Muslim*]

4.6 BENEFITS OF THE HADEETH

Aboo Hurayrah	
Closeness to Allah varies:	1 Time
	2 Situation
	3 Piety
The benefit of nearness	
Supplicating much	
"Asking too much?"	
Not asking Allah at all	
Hearts involved in prayer	
Prostrating after every prayer?	

4.7 ACTIVITY: Memorize this supplication to be used in the *"qunoot"* of *Witr* Prayer:

«اللّٰهُمَّ اهْدِنِي فِيمَنْ هَدَيْتَ، وَعَافِنِي فِيمَنْ عَافَيْتَ، وَتَوَلَّنِي فِيمَنْ تَوَلَّيْتَ، وَبَارِكْ لِي فِيمَا أَعْطَيْتَ، وَقِنِي شَرَّ مَا قَضَيْتَ، فَإِنَّكَ تَقْضِي وَلَا يُقْضَى عَلَيْكَ، وَإِنَّهُ لَا يَذِلُّ مَنْ وَالَيْتَ، وَلَا يَعِزُّ مَنْ عَادَيْتَ، تَبَارَكْتَ رَبَّنَا وَتَعَالَيْتَ.»

[أَخْرَجَهُ أَحْمَدُ وَأَصْحَابُ السُّنَنِ، وَصَحَّحَهُ الْأَلْبَانِيُّ فِي إِرْوَاءِ الغَلِيلِ برقم ٤٢٩]

"O Allah, guide me among those whom You have guided. Give me well-being from those whom You have given well-being. Accept me as an ally among those whom You have taken as allies. Bless me among those whom You have blessed. Save me from the evil of what You have decreed, as You (alone) decree (everything), and no decree is issued over You. Certainly, no ally of Yours is disgraced, and none whom you oppose attain honor. Blessed are You, our Lord, in Lofty Exaltation."

[Collected by Ahmad and the authors of the *Sunan* compilations. Declared authentic by al-Albaanee in *Irwaa' al-Ghaleel, no. 429.*]

5.1 QURAN STUDY

أُحِلَّ لَكُمْ لَيْلَةَ الصِّيَامِ الرَّفَثُ إِلَىٰ نِسَآئِكُمْ هُنَّ لِبَاسٌ لَّكُمْ وَأَنتُمْ لِبَاسٌ لَّهُنَّ عَلِمَ اللَّهُ أَنَّكُمْ كُنتُمْ تَخْتَانُونَ أَنفُسَكُمْ فَتَابَ عَلَيْكُمْ وَعَفَا عَنكُمْ فَالْـَٰنَ بَـٰشِرُوهُنَّ وَابْتَغُواْ مَا كَتَبَ اللَّهُ لَكُمْ وَكُلُواْ وَاشْرَبُواْ حَتَّىٰ يَتَبَيَّنَ لَكُمُ الْخَيْطُ الْأَبْيَضُ مِنَ الْخَيْطِ الْأَسْوَدِ مِنَ الْفَجْرِ ثُمَّ أَتِمُّواْ الصِّيَامَ إِلَى الَّيْلِ وَلَا تُبَـٰشِرُوهُنَّ وَأَنتُمْ عَـٰكِفُونَ فِي الْمَسَـٰجِدِ تِلْكَ حُدُودُ اللَّهِ فَلَا تَقْرَبُوهَا كَذَٰلِكَ يُبَيِّنُ اللَّهُ ءَايَـٰتِهِ لِلنَّاسِ لَعَلَّهُمْ يَتَّقُونَ ﴿ البقرة: ١٨٧ ﴾

"Permissible for you during the nights of fasting is intimacy with your women. They are garments for you, and you are garments for them. Allah knew you had been betraying yourselves, so He accepted your repentance and excused you. Now you may touch them (intimately) and seek after what Allah has written for you. Eat and drink until the white thread of dawn becomes clear to you from the dark thread [of night]. Then, complete the fast until nightfall. And do not touch them (intimately) whilst you are performing *i'tikaaf* in the masjids. These are the limits of Allah, so do not transgress them. Thus Allah does clarify His Verses for the people, so they may have *taqwa* [being conscious and fearful of Him]." [2:187]

23

5.2 VOCABULARY OF THE VERSE

الرَّفَثُ إِلَى نِسَائِكُمْ	لَيْلَةَ الصِّيَامِ	أُحِلَّ لَكُمْ
فَتَابَ عَلَيْكُمْ	تَخْتَانُونَ أَنْفُسَكُمْ	لِبَاسٌ
وَكُلُوا وَاشْرَبُوا	بَاشِرُوهُنَّ	وَعَفَا عَنْكُمْ
الخَيْطِ الأَسْوَدِ	الخَيْطُ الأَبْيَضُ	حَتَّى يَتَبَيَّنَ لَكُمْ
إِلَى اللَّيْلِ	أَتِمُّوا الصِّيَامَ	مِنَ الفَجْرِ
فِي المَسَاجِدِ	وَأَنْتُمْ عَاكِفُونَ	وَلَا تُبَاشِرُوهُنَّ
لَعَلَّهُمْ يَتَّقُونَ	فَلَا تَقْرَبُوهَا	حُدُودُ اللهِ

5.3 AN ARABIC LANGUAGE ACTIVITY

Locate the Arabic wordings for the following commands and prohibitions in the Verse:

Touch them (intimately)	﴿بَاشِرُوهُنَّ﴾
And seek after	
And eat	
And drink	
Complete the fast	
And do not touch them (intimately)	
So do not approach them	

5.4 TAFSEER BENEFITS

Definition of the night	Begins:
	Ends:
Permissible actions at night	1
	2
	3
Closeness of spouses	
Definition of *i'tikaaf*	
Not transgressing Allah's Limits	
The goal of fasting revisited	

5.5 HADEETH STUDY

عَنْ عَبْدِ اللهِ بْنِ أَبِي أَوْفَى رَضِيَ اللهُ عَنْهُ، قَالَ: كُنْتُ مَعَ النَّبِيِّ صَلَّى اللهُ عَلَيْهِ وَسَلَّمَ فِي سَفَرٍ، فَصَامَ حَتَّى أَمْسَى، قَالَ لِرَجُلٍ: «انْزِلْ، فَاجْدَحْ لِي!» قَالَ: لَوِ انْتَظَرْتَ حَتَّى تُمْسِيَ؟ قَالَ: «انْزِلْ، فَاجْدَحْ لِـي، إِذَا رَأَيْتَ اللَّيْلَ قَدْ أَقْبَلَ مِنْ هَا هُنَا، فَقَدْ أَفْطَرَ الصَّائِمُ»

[مُتَّفَقٌ عَلَيْهِ]

'Abdullah ibn Abee Owfaa (may Allah be pleased with him) said: I was with the Prophet (may Allah raise his rank and grant him peace) during a journey, when he fasted until the evening. He said to a man, **"Stop and prepare my drink."** He replied, **"If you could wait until you reach the night?"** He said, **"Stop and prepare my drink. When you see the night approaching from over here, the fasting person has certainly broken his fast."** [*Agreed upon*]

25

5.6 BENEFITS OF THE HADEETH

'Abdullah ibn Abee Owfaa	
Fasting during a journey	
Breaking fast at sunset	
Teaching during a journey	
Teaching one's servant	
Leadership during journeys	

5.7 RESEARCH: Locate this hadeeth in *Saheeh al-Bukhaaree*, in the chapters about fasting, specifically: the sub-chapter about hastening to break the fast. You should see another hadeeth in the same chapter, shorter in wording. What is the relationship between the two hadeeths?

6.1 QURAN STUDY

هُوَ ٱلَّذِىٓ أَنزَلَ عَلَيْكَ ٱلْكِتَـٰبَ مِنْهُ ءَايَـٰتٌ مُّحْكَمَـٰتٌ هُنَّ أُمُّ ٱلْكِتَـٰبِ وَأُخَرُ مُتَشَـٰبِهَـٰتٌ فَأَمَّا ٱلَّذِينَ فِى قُلُوبِهِمْ زَيْغٌ فَيَتَّبِعُونَ مَا تَشَـٰبَهَ مِنْهُ ٱبْتِغَآءَ ٱلْفِتْنَةِ وَٱبْتِغَآءَ تَأْوِيلِهِۦ وَمَا يَعْلَمُ تَأْوِيلَهُۥٓ إِلَّا ٱللَّهُ وَٱلرَّٰسِخُونَ فِى ٱلْعِلْمِ يَقُولُونَ ءَامَنَّا بِهِۦ كُلٌّ مِّنْ عِندِ رَبِّنَا وَمَا يَذَّكَّرُ إِلَّآ أُوْلُوا۟ ٱلْأَلْبَـٰبِ ﴿ آل عمران: ٧ ﴾

"He is the One who sent down to you the Book; in it are decisively clear Verses. They are the foundation of the Book. Others are not entirely clear. Those in whose hearts is deviation follow after what is not decisively clear of that, seeking *fitnah*, and seeking [false] explanations. Yet, none know their [true] explanations other than Allah. Those firmly grounded in knowledge say: 'We have believed in it; all of it is from our Lord.' Yet, none truly reflect other than people of understanding." [3:7]

6.2 VOCABULARY OF THE VERSE

الَّذِينَ فِي قُلُوبِهِمْ زَيْغٌ	وَأُخَرُ مُتَشَابِهَاتٌ	آيَاتٌ مُحْكَمَاتٌ
ابْتِغَاءَ الْفِتْنَةِ	مَا تَشَابَهَ مِنْهُ	فَيَتَّبِعُونَ
أُولُوا الْأَلْبَابِ	وَالرَّاسِخُونَ فِي الْعِلْمِ	وَابْتِغَاءَ تَأْوِيلِهِ

6.3 AN ARABIC LANGUAGE BENEFIT

Consider the verbs used in the examples below. Practice changing the verb as needed when switching from noun-based sentences (اسمية) to verb-based sentences (فعلية).

جُمْلَةٌ اسْمِيَّةٌ	جُمْلَةٌ فِعْلِيَّةٌ
﴿وَالرَّاسِخُونَ فِي الْعِلْمِ يَقُولُونَ ءَامَنَّا بِهِۦ﴾	وَيَقُولُ الرَّاسِخُونَ فِي العِلْمِ آمَنَّا بِهِ
الَّذِينَ فِي قُلُوبِهِمْ زَيْغٌ يَتَّبِعُونَ الْمُتَشَابِهَاتِ	_____ الَّذِينَ فِي قُلُوبِهِمْ زَيْغٌ الْمُتَشَابِهَاتِ
أُولُوا الْأَلْبَابِ _____	يَتَذَكَّرُ أُولُوا الْأَلْبَابِ
اللهُ أَنْزَلَ الكِتَابَ	

6.4 TAFSEER BENEFITS

Clear and unclear Verses	
Deviants read the Quran	
Methodology of deviants	1
	2
Methodology of *Ahlus-Sunnah*	1
	2
Two different recitations	
The place of intellect	

28

6.5 HADEETH STUDY

عَنْ عَائِشَةَ رَضِيَ اللهُ عَنْهَا، قَالَتْ: تَلَا رَسُولُ اللهِ صَلَّى اللهُ عَلَيْهِ وَسَلَّمَ: ﴿ هُوَ ٱلَّذِىٓ أَنزَلَ عَلَيْكَ ٱلْكِتَٰبَ مِنْهُ ءَايَٰتٌ مُّحْكَمَٰتٌ... ﴾ الآية، فَقَالَ: «إِذَا رَأَيْتُمُ الَّذِينَ يَتَّبِعُونَ مَا تَشَابَهَ مِنْهُ، فَأُولَٰئِكَ الَّذِينَ سَمَّى اللهُ، فَاحْذَرُوهُمْ!» [مُتَّفَقٌ عَلَيْهِ]

'Aa'ishah (may Allah be pleased with her) said: The Messenger of Allah (may Allah raise his rank and grant him peace) recited, **"He is the One who sent down to you the Book; in it are decisively clear Verses..."** and then said: **"When you see those who follow after what is unclear of it, those are the ones whom Allah has named, so be warned of them!"**
[Agreed upon]

6.6 BENEFITS OF THE HADEETH

'Aa'ishah	
Prophetic Tafseer	
Being on guard against deviants	
Warning others of deviants	
Quran put into action	

6.7 ACTIVITY: Memorize this supplication from *Soorah Aali 'Emraan*:

رَبَّنَا لَا تُزِغْ قُلُوبَنَا بَعْدَ إِذْ هَدَيْتَنَا وَهَبْ لَنَا مِن لَّدُنكَ رَحْمَةً إِنَّكَ أَنتَ ٱلْوَهَّابُ ۝

رَبَّنَا إِنَّكَ جَامِعُ ٱلنَّاسِ لِيَوْمٍ لَّا رَيْبَ فِيهِ إِنَّ ٱللَّهَ لَا يُخْلِفُ ٱلْمِيعَادَ ۝

"O our Lord! Do not send our hearts into deviation after You have guided us! And grant us from Yourself a portion of Mercy! Certainly, You are the Ever Bestowing! Our Lord! Certainly, You are the One who gathers the people unto a Day about which there is no doubt! Verily, Allah does not break His Promise!" [3:8-9]

7.1 QURAN STUDY

﴿ قُلْ يَا أَهْلَ الْكِتَابِ تَعَالَوْا إِلَى كَلِمَةٍ سَوَاءٍ بَيْنَنَا وَبَيْنَكُمْ أَلَّا نَعْبُدَ إِلَّا اللَّهَ وَلَا نُشْرِكَ بِهِ شَيْئًا وَلَا يَتَّخِذَ بَعْضُنَا بَعْضًا أَرْبَابًا مِّن دُونِ اللَّهِ فَإِن تَوَلَّوْا فَقُولُوا اشْهَدُوا بِأَنَّا مُسْلِمُونَ ﴾ آل عمران: ٦٤

"Say: 'O People of the Book! Come to a mutual word of agreement between us and you: That we do not worship but Allah, that we do not associate any partners with Him, and that we do not take one another as lords besides Allah.' If they turn away, then say: 'Be witnesses that we are Muslims.'" [3:64]

7.2 VOCABULARY OF THE VERSE

إِلَى كَلِمَةٍ	تَعَالَوْا	قُلْ يَا أَهْلَ الْكِتَابِ
وَلَا نُشْرِكَ بِهِ شَيْئًا	أَلَّا نَعْبُدَ إِلَّا اللهَ	سَوَاءٍ بَيْنَنَا وَبَيْنَكُمْ
فَإِنْ تَوَلَّوْا	أَرْبَابًا مِنْ دُونِ اللهِ	وَلَا يَتَّخِذَ بَعْضُنَا بَعْضًا
بِأَنَّا مُسْلِمُونَ	اشْهَدُوا	فَقُولُوا

7.3 AN ARABIC LANGUAGE BENEFIT

The word أَلَّا "Al-laa" is actually two words put together: أَنْ "An" + لا "Laa". Pay attention to the subtle differences between this phrase and some other words which closely resemble it. Try to find an example of each word in the Quran to complete the following table.

أَلَّا نَعْبُدَ إِلَّا اللهَ	← أَنْ لَا نَعْبُدَ إِلَّا اللهَ →	
إِلَّا [لِلاِسْتِثْنَاءِ]	أَلَا [لِلتَّنْبِيهِ]	أَلَّا = أَنْ لَا

	أَلَّا
	أَلَا
	إِلَّا

7.4 TAFSEER BENEFITS

People of the Book/Scripture	
Which of them are believers?	
Real "interfaith dialogue"	
The goal of coming together: Agreement on three basics	1
	2
	3
If they turn away	
If they embrace the message	

عَنِ ابْنِ عَبَّاسٍ رَضِيَ اللهُ عَنْهُمَا، قَالَ: لَمَّا بَعَثَ النَّبِيُّ صَلَّى اللهُ عَلَيْهِ

وَسَلَّمَ مُعَاذَ بْنَ جَبَلٍ إِلَى نَحْوِ أَهْلِ اليَمَنِ، قَالَ لَهُ: «إِنَّكَ تَقْدُمُ عَلَى

قَوْمٍ مِنْ أَهْلِ الكِتَابِ، فَلْيَكُنْ أَوَّلَ مَا تَدْعُوهُمْ إِلَى أَنْ يُوَحِّدُوا اللهَ

تَعَالَى، فَإِذَا عَرَفُوا ذَلِكَ، فَأَخْبِرْهُمْ أَنَّ اللهَ قَدْ فَرَضَ عَلَيْهِمْ خَمْسَ

صَلَوَاتٍ فِي يَوْمِهِمْ وَلَيْلَتِهِمْ، فَإِذَا صَلَّوْا، فَأَخْبِرْهُمْ أَنَّ اللهَ افْتَرَضَ

عَلَيْهِمْ زَكَاةً فِي أَمْوَالِهِمْ، تُؤْخَذُ مِنْ غَنِيِّهِمْ، فَتُرَدُّ عَلَى فَقِيرِهِمْ،

فَإِذَا أَقَرُّوا بِذلِكَ فَخُذْ مِنْهُمْ، وَتَوَقَّ كَرَائِمَ أَمْوَالِ النَّاسِ.»

[مُتَّفَقٌ عَلَيْهِ]

Ibn 'Abbaas (may Allah be pleased with him and his father) said: When the Prophet (may Allah raise his rank and grant him peace) sent Mu'aath ibn Jabal towards the people of Yemen, he said to him, **"You are approaching some of the people of the Book, so let the first thing you invite them to be: That they single out Allah, the Most High. If they know about that, then inform them that Allah has obliged them to pray five prayers throughout their day and night. If they pray, then inform them that Allah has obliged them to pay** *zakaat* **from their wealth; it is collected from their rich and redistributed to their poor. If they accept that, then take from them [their** *zakaat* **to distribute it], but avoid the people's prize possessions."** [Agreed upon]

7.6 BENEFITS OF THE HADEETH

Ibn 'Abbaas	
Mu'aath ibn Jabal	
Knowledge precedes action	
Priorities of Mu'aath's *da'wah*	1
	2
	3
	4
Strengthening local economy	
Justice, fairness, and balance	
Assigning teachers to areas	

7.7 RESEARCH: Learn about Mu'aath ibn Jabal's ancestry and roots. How was he connected to Yemen? Why was he selected to go there? What important conclusion(s) can be drawn from your findings?

8.1 QURAN STUDY

> وَمَن يُطِعِ اللَّهَ وَالرَّسُولَ فَأُولَٰئِكَ مَعَ الَّذِينَ أَنْعَمَ اللَّهُ عَلَيْهِم مِّنَ النَّبِيِّينَ وَالصِّدِّيقِينَ وَالشُّهَدَاءِ وَالصَّالِحِينَ وَحَسُنَ أُولَٰئِكَ رَفِيقًا ۝ ذَٰلِكَ الْفَضْلُ مِنَ اللَّهِ وَكَفَىٰ بِاللَّهِ عَلِيمًا ۝ النساء
>
> "And those who obey Allah and the Messenger, such are with those whom I have bestowed My Favor upon, from the Prophets, the devoutly believing, the martyrs, and the righteous. And what good company those are! Such is the [true] Bounty from Allah. And sufficient is Allah as One who knows all." [4:69-70]

8.2 VOCABULARY OF THE VERSES

الَّذِينَ أَنْعَمَ اللَّهُ عَلَيْهِم	مِنَ النَّبِيِّينَ	وَالصِّدِّيقِينَ
وَالشُّهَدَاءِ	وَالصَّالِحِينَ	وَحَسُنَ أُولَئِكَ رَفِيقًا
ذَلِكَ الْفَضْلُ	مِنَ اللَّهِ	وَكَفَى بِاللَّهِ عَلِيمًا

8.3 AN ARABIC LANGUAGE BENEFIT

There are two basic types of plural nouns in Arabic. The first one is a regular plural, in Arabic it is called: جمع سالم. Regular plurals have the suffix "-oon" or "-een" at the end of the singular version of that noun (for masculine nouns). Irregular plurals, (جمع تكسير), are when the basic structure of the singular noun is manipulated with additions or deletions. This Quranic passage we are studying has a number of plural nouns, as listed on the table below. Try to complete the table as much as you can.

جَمْعُ تَكْسِيرٍ Irregular plural	جَمْعُ سَالِمٌ Regular plural	اسْمٌ مُفْرَدٌ Singular noun (m.)
الأَنْبِيَاءُ	﴿ٱلنَّبِيِّـۧنَ﴾	النَّبِيّ
	﴿وَٱلصِّدِّيقِينَ﴾	الصِّدِّيق
﴿وَٱلشُّهَدَآءِ﴾		الشَّهِيد
	_____	الصَّالِح
_____		التَّاجِر
_____	الكَافِرُونَ	_____
الأُمَنَاءُ		_____
	الصَّائِمُونَ	_____

8.4 TAFSEER BENEFITS

Our creation is a test	
Obedient Muslims shall be in the company of those whom Allah has favored, the likes of:	1
	2
	3
	4
Definition of a Prophet	
Definition of a "siddeeq"	

36

Definition of a martyr	
Definition of a righteous man	
When/where is this companionship?	This life:
	The next:
Allah knows all hidden matters	
Claims of piety vs. true piety	
Tafseer of Quran by Quran	

8.5 HADEETH STUDY

عَنْ أَبِي سَعِيدٍ رَضِيَ اللهُ عَنْهُ، عَنِ النَّبِيِّ صَلَّى اللهُ عَلَيْهِ وَسَلَّمَ، قَالَ:

«التَّاجِرُ الصَّدُوقُ الأَمِينُ مَعَ النَّبِيِّينَ، وَالصِّدِّيقِينَ، وَالشُّهَدَاءِ.»

[أخرجه الترمذي وقال: حديث حسن، وحسَّنه لغيره صاحب السلسلة الصحيحة

برقم ٣٤٥٣ بعد أن كان يضعِّفه]

On the authority of Aboo Sa'eed (may Allah be pleased with him), from the Prophet (may Allah raise his rank and grant him peace), who said: **"The honest, trustworthy merchant is with the Prophets, the devoutly believing, and the martyrs."** [at-Tirmithee, authentic]

8.6 BENEFITS OF THE HADEETH

Aboo Sa'eed	
Traits of obedient servants	1
	2
Marketplaces in general	

37

Tafseer of Quran by Hadeeth	
Tafseer by specific example	

8.7 ACTIVITY: Memorize this important Prophetic supplication from *Saheeh Muslim*:

«اللّهُمَّ مُصَرِّفَ الْقُلُوبِ صَرِّفْ قُلُوبَنَا عَلَى طَاعَتِكَ»

"O Allah! Turner of the hearts! Turn our hearts upon Your Obedience!"

9.1 QURAN STUDY

﴿ وَإِذَا قِيلَ لَهُمْ تَعَالَوْا إِلَىٰ مَا أَنزَلَ ٱللَّهُ وَإِلَى ٱلرَّسُولِ قَالُوا۟ حَسْبُنَا مَا وَجَدْنَا عَلَيْهِ ءَابَآءَنَآ أَوَلَوْ كَانَ ءَابَآؤُهُمْ لَا يَعْلَمُونَ شَيْـًٔا وَلَا يَهْتَدُونَ ﴾ المائدة: ١٠٤

"And when it is said to them: 'Come to what Allah has sent down, and [come to] the Messenger,' They say: 'Sufficient for us is what we found our forefathers upon!' Even if their forefathers did not know anything, nor were they rightly guided!" [5:104]

9.2 VOCABULARY OF THE VERSE

إِلَى مَا أَنْزَلَ الله	تَعَالَوْا	وَإِذَا قِيلَ لَهُمْ
مَا وَجَدْنَا عَلَيْهِ آبَاءَنَا	حَسْبُنَا	وَإِلَى الرَّسُولِ
	وَلَا يَهْتَدُونَ	لَا يَعْلَمُونَ شَيْئًا

9.3 AN ARABIC LANGUAGE BENEFIT

Prepositions attach to pronouns to form single words. Consider the two examples of this in the Verse, and then practice this operation by completing the following table:

لِ + هُمْ = لَهُمْ	عَلَى + هُوَ = عَلَيْهِ
فِي + هِيَ = _____	بِ + ____ = بِهِمْ
مِن + هُنَّ = _____	إِلَى + ____ = إِلَيْنَا
____ + ____ = عَنْهُمَا	____ + ____ = عَلَيْكِ
____ + ____ = فِيكُم	____ + ____ = لَكَ

9.4 TAFSEER BENEFITS

Calling disbelievers to Islam	
Lofty status of the Messenger	
The way of the ancestors	
False excuses disproven	
What a terrible trade-in	

9.5 HADEETH STUDY

عَنِ الْمُسَيِّبِ رَضِيَ اللهُ عَنْهُ، أَنَّ أَبَا طَالِبٍ لَمَّا حَضَرَتْهُ الْوَفَاةُ، دَخَلَ عَلَيْهِ النَّبِيُّ صَلَّى اللهُ عَلَيْهِ وَسَلَّمَ وَعِنْدَهُ أَبُو جَهْلٍ، فَقَالَ: «أَيْ عَمِّ! قُلْ لَا إِلٰهَ إِلَّا اللهُ، كَلِمَةً أُحَاجُّ لَكَ بِهَا عِنْدَ اللهِ!» فَقَالَ أَبُو جَهْلٍ وَعَبْدُ اللهِ بْنُ أَبِي أُمَيَّةَ: يَا أَبَا طَالِبٍ! تَرْغَبُ عَنْ مِلَّةِ عَبْدِ الْمُطَّلِبِ؟ فَلَمْ يَزَالَا يُكَلِّمَانِهِ، حَتَّى قَالَ آخِرَ شَيْءٍ كَلَّمَهُمْ بِهِ: عَلَى مِلَّةِ عَبْدِ الْمُطَّلِبِ. [مُتَّفَقٌ عَلَيْهِ]

Al-Musayyib (may Allah be pleased with him) said: When Aboo Taalib was dying, the Prophet (may Allah raise his rank and grant him peace) went to him, while Aboo Jahl was there, and said, **"My uncle! Say: *Laa-ilaaha-ill-Allaah* (none deserve worship other than Allah), a word I could use to argue on your behalf with Allah!"** So Aboo Jahl and 'Abdullaah ibn Abee Umayyah said, "O Abaa Taalib! Are you inclined against the religion of 'Abdul-Muttalib?" And they went on talking to him (like this) until the last thing he said to them (before dying) was that he was upon the religion of 'Abdul-Muttalib. [Agreed upon]

9.6 BENEFITS OF THE HADEETH

Al-Musayyib	
Aboo Taalib	
Aboo Jahl	
'Abdullaah ibn Abee Umayyah	
'Abdul-Muttalib	
Prophetic *da'wah*	
Intercession (for whom)	

Bad companionship	
The polytheists angle of *da'wah*	
Over-attachment to ancestors	
Aiding Islam but not accepting it	

9.7 RESEARCH: What does a Muslim say as a regular phrase of *thikr* (remembrance) which begins with **"Hasbunaa..."** as found in the Quran (3:173)?

Based on the context of the Verse, in what kind of real life situations would you say this phrase?

10.1 QURAN STUDY

﴿ وَهُوَ ٱلَّذِى جَعَلَكُمْ خَلَٰٓئِفَ ٱلْأَرْضِ وَرَفَعَ بَعْضَكُمْ فَوْقَ بَعْضٍ دَرَجَٰتٍ لِّيَبْلُوَكُمْ فِى مَآ ءَاتَىٰكُمْ ۗ إِنَّ رَبَّكَ سَرِيعُ ٱلْعِقَابِ وَإِنَّهُۥ لَغَفُورٌ رَّحِيمٌ ﴾ الأنعام: ١٦٥

"And He is the One who made you successors in the land, and He raised some of you over others in rank, in order to test you with what He has given you. Certainly, your Lord is swift in punishment. And certainly, He is the Oft-Forgiving, the Ever Merciful." [6:165]

10.2 VOCABULARY OF THE VERSE

خَلَائِفَ الأَرْضِ	جَعَلَكُمْ	وَهُوَ الَّذِي
دَرَجَاتٍ	فَوْقَ بَعْضٍ	وَرَفَعَ بَعْضَكُمْ
إِنَّ رَبَّكَ	فِي مَا آتَاكُمْ	لِيَبْلُوَكُمْ
رَحِيمٌ	وَإِنَّهُ لَغَفُورٌ	سَرِيعُ العِقَابِ

10.3 AN ARABIC LANGUAGE BENEFIT

Each pronoun has an appropriate *"ism mowsool"* that goes with it, as detailed in the table. The pronoun, followed by its *"ism mowsool"* is often used to identify people or things and their characteristics. Consider the examples provided in the table. Look for these phrases in your reading of the Quran. Complete the missing fields, using the references provided.

﴿وَهُوَ ٱلَّذِى جَعَلَكُمْ خَلَٰئِفَ ٱلْأَرْضِ﴾ الأنعام: ١٦٥	الَّذِي	هُوَ
﴿ٱلَّتِى تَطَّلِعُ عَلَى ٱلْأَفْـِٔدَةِ﴾ الهمزة: ٧	الَّتِي	هِيَ
﴿ـــــــ يَأْتِيَٰنِهَا مِنكُمْ فَـَٔاذُوهُمَا﴾ النساء: ١٦	الَّذَانِ	هُمَا
"مَنِ الْمَرْأَتَانِ اللَّتَانِ تَظَاهَرَتَا؟" [متفق عليه]	اللَّتَانِ	هُمَا
﴿ـــــــ يَقُولُونَ لَا تُنفِقُوا﴾ المنافقون: ٧	الَّذِينَ	هُمْ
﴿ ﴾ المجادلة: ٢	اللَّائِي	هُنَّ
﴿ ﴾ يوسف: ٥٠	اللَّاتِي	هُنَّ

10.4 TAFSEER BENEFITS

Allah reminds us of His Favors	
Varieties of distinctions	16:70
	16:71
	16:72
	16:73
	Soorah an-Nahl is also called:
Unequal distribution as a test	
Allah is swift in punishment	
Allah is Forgiving and Merciful	
Derived: Allah's Justice	

10.5 HADEETH STUDY

عَنْ أَبِي هُرَيْرَةَ رَضِيَ اللهُ عَنْهُ: أَنَّ رَسُولَ اللهِ صَلَّى اللهُ عَلَيْهِ وَسَلَّمَ قَالَ:

«لاَ حَسَدَ إِلَّا فِي اثْنَتَيْنِ: رَجُلٌ عَلَّمَهُ اللهُ الْقُرْآنَ، فَهُوَ يَتْلُوهُ آنَاءَ

اللَّيْلِ، وَآنَاءَ النَّهَارِ، فَسَمِعَهُ جَارٌ لَهُ، فَقَالَ: لَيْتَنِي أُوتِيتُ مِثْلَ مَا

أُوتِيَ فُلَانٌ، فَعَمِلْتُ مِثْلَ مَا يَعْمَلُ؛ وَرَجُلٌ آتَاهُ اللهُ مَالًا، فَهُوَ

يُهْلِكُهُ فِي الْحَقِّ، فَقَالَ رَجُلٌ: لَيْتَنِي أُوتِيتُ مِثْلَ مَا أُوتِيَ فُلَانٌ،

فَعَمِلْتُ مِثْلَ مَا يَعْمَلُ!» [مُتَّفَقٌ عَلَيْهِ]

On the authority of Aboo Hurayrah (may Allah be pleased with him): The Messenger of Allah (may Allah raise his rank and grant him peace) said, **"There is no jealousy except in two [cases]: [1] A man whom Allah has taught the Quran, and he recites it at all hours of the day and night. A neighbor hears him and says: 'I wish I could be given what So-and-So has, so I could do what he does.' [2] A man whom Allah has given wealth, and he spends it all in the [way of the] Truth. A man says: 'I wish I had what So-and-Son has been given, so I could do what he does!'"** [Agreed upon]

10.6 BENEFITS OF THE HADEETH

Aboo Hurayrah	
Prohibition of envy	
At the core of forbidden envy	
"Ghibtah" (beneficial jealousy)	
Two virtuous people, whom we should be jealous of	1
	2

45

10.7 RESOURCE: Some things you can say when you see something admirable about other Muslims:

بَارَكَ اللهُ فِيْكُمْ	بَارَكَ اللهُ فِيْكِ	بَارَكَ اللهُ فِيْكَ
بَارَكَ اللهُ فِيْهِمْ	بَارَكَ اللهُ فِيْهَا	بَارَكَ اللهُ فِيْهِ
اللّهُمَّ بَارِكْ لَكُمْ	اللّهُمَّ بَارِكْ لَكِ	اللّهُمَّ بَارِكْ لَكَ
اللّهُمَّ بَارِكْ لَهُمْ	اللّهُمَّ بَارِكْ لَهَا	اللّهُمَّ بَارِكْ لَهُ

(This is based on the general Prophetic guidance to supplicate for barakah (blessings) when you see something about your brother which impresses you.)

11.1 QURAN STUDY

﴿ ٱلَّذِينَ يَتَّبِعُونَ ٱلرَّسُولَ ٱلنَّبِيَّ ٱلْأُمِّيَّ ٱلَّذِى يَجِدُونَهُ مَكْتُوبًا عِندَهُمْ فِى ٱلتَّوْرَىٰةِ وَٱلْإِنجِيلِ يَأْمُرُهُم بِٱلْمَعْرُوفِ وَيَنْهَىٰهُمْ عَنِ ٱلْمُنكَرِ وَيُحِلُّ لَهُمُ ٱلطَّيِّبَٰتِ وَيُحَرِّمُ عَلَيْهِمُ ٱلْخَبَٰئِثَ وَيَضَعُ عَنْهُمْ إِصْرَهُمْ وَٱلْأَغْلَٰلَ ٱلَّتِى كَانَتْ عَلَيْهِمْ فَٱلَّذِينَ ءَامَنُوا۟ بِهِۦ وَعَزَّرُوهُ وَنَصَرُوهُ وَٱتَّبَعُوا۟ ٱلنُّورَ ٱلَّذِى أُنزِلَ مَعَهُۥٓ أُو۟لَٰئِكَ هُمُ ٱلْمُفْلِحُونَ ﴾ الأعراف: ١٥٧

"Those who follow the Messenger, the unlettered Prophet, whom they find written with them in the Torah and *Injeel*, he orders them with good and forbids them from evil, and he allows them to have wholesome things and forbids them from filthy things. He removes the difficult burdens and restrictions that were upon them. So those who believe in, honor, and support him, and they follow the Light which has been sent down with him, such are the successful ones." [7:157]

11.2 VOCABULARY OF THE VERSE

يَتَّبِعُونَ	الْأُمِّيَّ	يَجِدُونَهُ
مَكْتُوبًا عِنْدَهُمْ	التَّوْرَاةِ	الْإِنْجِيلِ

ويُحِلُّ لَهُمُ الطَّيِّبَاتِ	وَيَنْهَاهُمْ عَنِ الْمُنْكَرِ	يَأْمُرُهُمْ بِالْمَعْرُوفِ
وَالْأَغْلَالَ	وَيَضَعُ عَنْهُمْ إِصْرَهُمْ	وَيُحَرِّمُ عَلَيْهِمُ الْخَبَائِثَ
الْمُفْلِحُونَ	وَنَصَرُوهُ	وَعَزَّرُوهُ

11.3 AN ARABIC LANGUAGE BENEFIT

In this Verse, the Messenger of Allah (may Allah raise his rank and grant him peace) is described with five present tense verb phrases. Read the summary of those verb phrases in the following table, then add other descriptions of our Prophet (may Allah raise his rank and grant him peace) that come as present tense verb phrases from other passages in the Quran.

Verse	Meaning	Passage
7:157	Orders them with good	﴿ يَأْمُرُهُم بِالْمَعْرُوفِ ﴾
7:157	Forbids them from evil	﴿ وَيَنْهَاهُمْ عَنِ الْمُنكَرِ ﴾
7:157	Declares good things *halaal*	﴿ وَيُحِلُّ لَهُمُ الطَّيِّبَاتِ ﴾
7:157	Declares filthy things *haraam*	﴿ وَيُحَرِّمُ عَلَيْهِمُ الْخَبَائِثَ ﴾
7:157	Removes burdens & restrictions	﴿ وَيَضَعُ عَنْهُمْ إِصْرَهُمْ وَالْأَغْلَالَ ﴾
3:164		
3:164		
3:164		

11.4 TAFSEER BENEFITS

Definition of a Messenger		
Definition of a Prophet		
Unlettered/illiterate		
The Torah		
The *Injeel*		
His advent has been foretold		
His mission summarized in five main objectives	1	
	2	
	3	
	4	
	5	
Attributes of the successful	1	
	2	
	3	
	4	

11.5 HADEETH STUDY

عَنْ عَائِشَةَ رَضِيَ اللَّهُ عَنْهَا، قَالَتْ: "...فَرَجَعَ النَّبِيُّ صَلَّى اللهُ عَلَيْهِ وَسَلَّمَ إِلَى خَدِيجَةَ يَرْجُفُ فُؤَادُهُ، فَانْطَلَقَتْ بِهِ إِلَى وَرَقَةَ بْنِ نَوْفَلٍ، وَكَانَ رَجُلًا تَنَصَّرَ، يَقْرَأُ الْإِنْجِيلَ بِالْعَرَبِيَّةِ، فَقَالَ: مَاذَا تَرَى؟ فَأَخْبَرَهُ، فَقَالَ وَرَقَةُ: هَذَا النَّامُوسُ الَّذِي أَنْزَلَ اللَّهُ عَلَى مُوسَى، وَإِنْ أَدْرَكَنِي يَوْمُكَ أَنْصُرْكَ نَصْرًا مُؤَزَّرًا!" [مُتَّفَقٌ عَلَيْهِ]

On the authority of 'Aa'ishah (may Allah be pleased with her): "...Then the Prophet (may Allah raise his rank and grant him peace) returned to Khadeejah, his chest shaking [in fear]. She went with him to Waraqah ibn Nowfal, a man who had become a Christian who would read the *Injeel* in Arabic. He said, 'What have you seen?' So he told him. Waraqah then said, 'That is the *Naamoos* (Bringer of Revelation) which Allah sent down upon Moses. If I live to your time, I will certainly support you with great dedicated support!'" [Agreed upon]

11.6 BENEFITS OF THE HADEETH

'Aa'ishah	
Khadeejah	
Waraqah	
The events before this account	
Moses	
Revelation was anticipated	
The events after this account	

11.7 RESEARCH: Some scholars mention that Khadeejah was the best of our Prophet's wives. Others say that 'Aa'ishah was. What is correct about this?

FROM THE MANY FRUITS OF TAQWA

12.1 QURAN STUDY

يَٰٓأَيُّهَا ٱلَّذِينَ ءَامَنُوٓاْ إِن تَتَّقُواْ ٱللَّهَ يَجْعَل لَّكُمْ فُرْقَانًا وَيُكَفِّرْ عَنكُمْ سَيِّـَٔاتِكُمْ وَيَغْفِرْ لَكُمْ ۗ وَٱللَّهُ ذُو ٱلْفَضْلِ ٱلْعَظِيمِ ۝ الأنفال: ٢٩

"O you who have believed! If you fear Allah, He shall provide you with a criterion, expiate for you your sins, and forgive you. And Allah is the Owner of the Greatest Bounty." [8:29]

12.2 VOCABULARY OF THE VERSE

إِنْ تَتَّقُوا اللهَ	يَجْعَلْ لَكُمْ فُرْقَانًا	وَيُكَفِّرْ عَنْكُمْ سَيِّئَاتِكُمْ
وَيَغْفِرْ لَكُمْ	ذُو الفَضْلِ العَظِيمِ	

12.3 AN ARABIC LANGUAGE BENEFIT

The conditional clause, إِنْ (if/when), comes with two verbs: the condition and its fulfillment. In the meaning of the Verse: **IF** you fear Allah, He will provide a criterion. In this kind of construction, both present tense verbs come in the *majzoom* case, as illustrated in the examples in the following table. Take note of how the present tense verbs change from *marfoo'* to *majzoom*. Then, try to add in the final examples yourself.

Adding "IN" (verbs are *majzoom*)	Two verbs (*marfoo'* by default)
﴿إِن تَتَّقُوا۟ ٱللَّهَ يَجْعَل لَّكُمْ فُرْقَانًا﴾	تَتَّقُونَ اللهَ + يَجْعَلُ لَكُمْ فُرْقَانًا
﴿إِن تَنصُرُوا۟ ٱللَّهَ يَنصُرْكُمْ﴾ محمد: ٧	تَنْصُرُونَ اللهَ + يَنْصُرُكُمْ
﴿وَإِن تُبْدُوا۟ مَا فِىٓ أَنفُسِكُمْ أَوْ تُخْفُوهُ يُحَاسِبْكُم بِهِ ٱللَّهُ﴾ البقرة: ٢٨٤	تُبْدُونَ مَا فِي أَنْفُسِكُمْ أَوْ تُخْفُوهُ + يُحَاسِبُكُمْ بِهِ اللهُ
﴿ ﴾ النساء: ١٣٣	يَشَاءُ + يُذْهِبْكُم
﴿إِن يَشَأْ يَرْحَمْكُمْ﴾ الإسراء: ٥٤	_____ + _____
﴿إِن يَشَأْ يُعَذِّبْكُمْ﴾ الإسراء: ٥٤	_____ + _____

12.4 TAFSEER BENEFITS

The call: "O you who believe…"		
Definition of *taqwa*		
The condition & its fulfillment	Condition:	
	Fulfillment 1:	
	Fulfillment 2:	
	Fulfillment 3:	
Piety brings about clarity		
Neglect brings about confusion		
The expiation of sins		
Forgiveness from Allah		
The Great Bounty of Allah		
Ramadhan, the month of *taqwa*		

12.5 HADEETH STUDY

عَنْ حُذَيْفَةَ رَضِيَ اللهُ عَنْهُ، قَالَ: سَمِعْتُ رَسُولَ اللهِ صَلَّى اللهُ عَلَيْهِ وَسَلَّمَ يَقُولُ: «تُعْرَضُ الْفِتَنُ عَلَى الْقُلُوبِ، كَالْحَصِيرِ عُودًا عُودًا، فَأَيُّ قَلْبٍ أُشْرِبَهَا، نُكِتَ فِيهِ نُكْتَةٌ سَوْدَاءُ، وَأَيُّ قَلْبٍ أَنْكَرَهَا، نُكِتَ فِيهِ نُكْتَةٌ بَيْضَاءُ، حَتَّى تَصِيرَ عَلَى قَلْبَيْنِ، عَلَى أَبْيَضَ مِثْلِ الصَّفَا، فَلَا تَضُرُّهُ فِتْنَةٌ مَا دَامَتِ السَّمَاوَاتُ وَالْأَرْضُ، وَالْآخَرُ أَسْوَدُ مُرْبَادًّا كَالْكُوزِ مُجَخِّيًا، لَا يَعْرِفُ مَعْرُوفًا، وَلَا يُنْكِرُ مُنْكَرًا، إِلَّا مَا أُشْرِبَ مِنْ هَوَاهُ» [أَخْرَجَهُ مُسْلِمٌ]

On the authority of Huthayfah (may Allah be pleased with him), who said: I heard the Messenger of Allah (may Allah raise his rank and grant him peace) saying, **"Trials are continuously brought to the hearts, like [the continuous pattern of] straw fibers in a reed mat. Any heart that takes that in shall have a dark speck placed on it. Any heart that rejects that shall have a bright speck placed on it. Then, the hearts become of two types: [1] One is gleaming, like a smooth white rock, no trials harm it so long as the heavens and earth are still in place. [2] The other is dark, a pitch black night, like an overturned cup. It does not recognize any good, nor does it detest any evil. It is only inclined towards the desires it has taken in."** [Saheeh Muslim]

12.6 BENEFITS OF THE HADEETH

Huthayfah	
The importance of this hadeeth	
Trials of the heart	
Effects of embracing desires	1

53

	2	
	3	
	4	
Effects of rejecting desires	1	
	2	
	3	
	4	
Connection to the Verse (8:29)		
Eemaan increases & decreases		
Opportunities in Ramadhaan		

12.7 ACTIVITY: Gather examples of things the people differ over which have been clarified in *al-Furqaan* (the Quran), like the example provided.

People are confused about:	Al-Furqaan has clarified:
Jesus' identity (Lord, son of Lord...?)	Jesus was a Prophet
Jesus was left to die on the cross...?	

54

13.1 QURAN STUDY

﴿ إِنَّ عِدَّةَ ٱلشُّهُورِ عِندَ ٱللَّهِ ٱثْنَا عَشَرَ شَهْرًا فِى كِتَٰبِ ٱللَّهِ يَوْمَ خَلَقَ ٱلسَّمَٰوَٰتِ وَٱلْأَرْضَ مِنْهَآ أَرْبَعَةٌ حُرُمٌ ذَٰلِكَ ٱلدِّينُ ٱلْقَيِّمُ فَلَا تَظْلِمُوا۟ فِيهِنَّ أَنفُسَكُمْ وَقَٰتِلُوا۟ ٱلْمُشْرِكِينَ كَآفَّةً كَمَا يُقَٰتِلُونَكُمْ كَآفَّةً وَٱعْلَمُوٓا۟ أَنَّ ٱللَّهَ مَعَ ٱلْمُتَّقِينَ ﴾ التوبة: ٣٦

"Verily, the number of months with Allaah is twelve, in the Book of Allah, on the day He created the heavens and the earth. Of them, four are sacred. That is the upright Religion. So do not oppress yourselves in them (the months). And engage the polytheists in battle collectively, as they engage you in battle collectively. And know that Allah is with the pious." [9:36]

13.2 VOCABULARY OF THE VERSE

إِنَّ عِدَّةَ الشُّهُورِ	اثْنَا عَشَرَ شَهْرًا	أَرْبَعَةٌ حُرُمٌ
الدِّينُ القَيِّمُ	وَقَاتِلُوا المُشْرِكِينَ	كَافَّةً

13.3 AN ARABIC VOCABULARY BENEFIT

Learn the names of the months in Arabic, in order, as found in the following table. Also, note and remember which months are sacred (■), and which ones are months of Hajj (✸).

	٧	رَجَب ■		١	[الـ]مُحَرَّم ■
	٨	شَعْبَان		٢	صَفَر
	٩	رَمَضَان		٣	رَبِيعٌ الأَوَّلُ
	١٠	شَوَّال ✸		٤	رَبِيعٌ الآخَر [الثَّانِي]
	١١	ذُو القِعْدَة ✸ ■		٥	جُمَادَى الأُولَى
	١٢	ذُو الحِجَّة ✸ ■		٦	جُمَادَى الآخِرَة [الثَّانِية]

13.4 TAFSEER BENEFITS

Islamic calendar in the Quran			
A truly ancient calendar			
"In the Book of Allah"?			
The four sacred months	1		
	2		
	3		
	4		
The meaning of "sacred"			
Prohibition of self-oppression			
Engaging polytheists militarily			
The "Ma'iyyah" of Allah			
Taqwa defined & emphasized			

13.5 HADEETH STUDY

عَنْ أَبِي بَكْرَةَ رَضِيَ اللهُ عَنْهُ، عَنِ النَّبِيِّ صَلَّى اللهُ عَلَيْهِ وَسَلَّمَ، قَالَ:

«إِنَّ الزَّمَانَ قَدِ اسْتَدَارَ كَهَيْئَتِهِ يَوْمَ خَلَقَ اللهُ السَّمَاوَاتِ وَالأَرْضَ، السَّنَةُ اثْنَا عَشَرَ شَهْرًا، مِنْهَا أَرْبَعَةٌ حُرُمٌ، ثَلَاثٌ مُتَوَالِيَاتٌ: ذُو الْقَعْدَةِ، وَذُو الْحِجَّةِ، وَالْمُحَرَّمُ، وَرَجَبُ مُضَرَ الَّذِي بَيْنَ جُمَادَى وَشَعْبَانَ.» [مُتَّفَقٌ عَلَيْهِ]

On the authority of Aboo Bakrah (may Allah be pleased with him), from the Prophet (may Allah raise his rank and grant him peace), who said: **"Verily, time has come around full circle, like it was when Allah created the heavens and the earth. The year is twelve months, of which four are sacred. Three of them are consecutive:** *Thul-Qa'dah, Thul-Hijjah,* **and** *al-Muharram.* **Also, [the fourth one is] [the Tribe of] Mudhar's** *Rajab,* **the one between** *Jumaadaa* **and** *Sha'baan.***"** [Agreed upon]

13.6 BENEFITS OF THE HADEETH

Aboo Bakrah	
The context of this hadeeth	
Time has come around full circle	
3 consecutive sacred months	11
	12
	1
The other one	7

57

13.7 ACTIVITY: Adopt a practical way to connect to the Islamic calendar at least once every day, and never let it slip away from you! Share your idea(s).

ALLAH SEES AND KNOWS ALL THAT WE DO

14.1 QURAN STUDY

وَمَا تَكُونُ فِي شَأْنٍ وَمَا تَتْلُوا۟ مِنْهُ مِن قُرْءَانٍ وَلَا تَعْمَلُونَ مِنْ عَمَلٍ إِلَّا كُنَّا عَلَيْكُمْ شُهُودًا إِذْ تُفِيضُونَ فِيهِ وَمَا يَعْزُبُ عَن رَّبِّكَ مِن مِّثْقَالِ ذَرَّةٍ فِي ٱلْأَرْضِ وَلَا فِي ٱلسَّمَآءِ وَلَآ أَصْغَرَ مِن ذَٰلِكَ وَلَآ أَكْبَرَ إِلَّا فِي كِتَٰبٍ مُّبِينٍ ۞ يونس: ٦١

"No matter your situation, nothing do you recite of Quran, and no action at all do you perform, except that We are over you, in Witness, when you do it. Not the smallest grain on earth nor in the heavens is hidden from your Lord, and nothing even smaller than that, and nothing larger, except that it is in a clear written record." [10:61]

14.2 VOCABULARY OF THE VERSE

كُنَّا عَلَيْكُمْ شُهُودًا	وَمَا تَتْلُو	وَمَا تَكُونُ فِي شَأْنٍ
مِنْ مِثْقَالِ ذَرَّةٍ	وَمَا يَعْزُبُ عَنْ رَبِّكَ	إِذْ تُفِيضُونَ فِيهِ
كِتَابٍ مُبِينٍ	وَلَا أَكْبَرَ	وَلَا أَصْغَرَ

14.3 AN ARABIC LANGUAGE BENEFIT

Consider the all-inclusive negations followed by exclusive exemptions in this Verse, as identified in the following table. Linguists explain that this technique is the most expressive way to emphasize singularity and exclusivity. It is, after all, the technique used in the most important negation and affirmation of all: *Laa-ilaaha-ill-Allaah*, there exists no one who deserves any kind of worship, except Allah. Add the missing affirmations to the table from the last 30ᵗʰ of the Quran.

(The Affirmation) الإِثْبَاتُ	(The Negation) النَّفْيُ
	﴿ وَمَا تَكُونُ فِي شَأْنٍ ﴾
﴿ إِلَّا كُنَّا عَلَيْكُمْ شُهُودًا ﴾	﴿ وَمَا تَتْلُواْ مِنْهُ مِن قُرْءَانٍ ﴾
	﴿ وَلَا تَعْمَلُونَ مِنْ عَمَلٍ ﴾
﴿ إِلَّا فِي كِتَٰبٍ مُّبِينٍ ﴾	﴿ وَمَا يَعْزُبُ عَن رَّبِّكَ مِن مِّثْقَالِ ذَرَّةٍ ﴾
﴿ إِلَّا ٱللَّهَ ﴾	﴿ لَا إِلَٰهَ ﴾
﴿ إِلَّا لِيَعْبُدُواْ ٱللَّهَ مُخْلِصِينَ لَهُ ٱلدِّينَ ﴾	﴿ وَمَا أُمِرُواْ ﴾
	﴿ لَّيْسَ لَهُمْ طَعَامٌ ﴾
	﴿ لَا يَصْلَىٰهَآ ﴾
	﴿ وَمَا يُكَذِّبُ بِهِ ﴾
	﴿ فَذُوقُواْ فَلَن نَّزِيدَكُمْ ﴾

14.4 TAFSEER BENEFITS

No matter what your situation	
Allah is a Witness over you	
Every matter is already written	
The 4 stages of *Qadr* (review)	1
	2
	3
	4

Knowledge paired with writing	
The result: *taqwa* in our actions	

14.5 HADEETH STUDY

عَنْ أَبِي هُرَيْرَةَ رَضِيَ اللهُ عَنْهُ، قَالَ: كَانَ النَّبِيُّ صَلَّى اللهُ عَلَيْهِ وَسَلَّمَ
بَارِزًا يَوْمًا لِلنَّاسِ، فَأَتَاهُ جِبْرِيلُ، فَقَالَ: مَا الإِيمَانُ؟ قَالَ: «الإِيمَانُ
أَنْ تُؤْمِنَ بِاللهِ وَمَلَائِكَتِهِ، وَكُتُبِهِ، وَبِلِقَائِهِ، وَرُسُلِهِ وَتُؤْمِنَ بِالْبَعْثِ.»
قَالَ: مَا الإِسْلَامُ؟ قَالَ: «الإِسْلَامُ: أَنْ تَعْبُدَ اللهَ، وَلَا تُشْرِكَ بِهِ شَيْئًا،
وَتُقِيمَ الصَّلَاةَ، وَتُؤَدِّيَ الزَّكَاةَ الْمَفْرُوضَةَ، وَتَصُومَ رَمَضَانَ.» قَالَ:
مَا الإِحْسَانُ؟ قَالَ: «أَنْ تَعْبُدَ اللهَ كَأَنَّكَ تَرَاهُ، فَإِنْ لَمْ تَكُنْ تَرَاهُ فَإِنَّهُ
يَرَاكَ...» [مُتَّفَقٌ عَلَيْهِ]

On the authority of Aboo Hurayrah (may Allah be pleased with him) who said: One day, the Prophet (may Allah raise his rank and grant him peace), was out with the people, when Jibreel came and said, "What is *eemaan*?" He replied, **"It is to believe in Allah, His Angels, His Books, His Meeting, His Messengers, and to believe in the Resurrection."** He then asked, "What is Islam? He replied, **"It is to worship Allah and to not set up any partners unto Him, to establish the prayer, discharge the obligatory *zakaat*, and to fast in Ramadhaan."** He then asked, "What is *ihsaan*?" He replied, **"It is to worship Allah as if you see Him, yet when you do not actually see Him, then certainly [you know] He sees you..."** [Agreed upon]

14.6 BENEFITS OF THE HADEETH

Aboo Hurayrah	
This famous hadeeth	
A pillar of *eemaan* unmentioned	
A pillar of Islam unmentioned	
Ihsaan is the pinnacle of piety	

14.7 ACTIVITY: The scholars say the hadeeth of Jibreel, when **"He came to teach you your Religion,"** is an amazing series of beneficial lessons in manners. Try to list all of the points about manners you find in the hadeeth.

15.1 QURAN STUDY

﴿ قُل هَٰذِهِۦ سَبِيلِىٓ أَدْعُوٓاْ إِلَى ٱللَّهِ عَلَىٰ بَصِيرَةٍ أَنَا۠ وَمَنِ ٱتَّبَعَنِى وَسُبْحَٰنَ ٱللَّهِ وَمَآ أَنَا۠ مِنَ ٱلْمُشْرِكِينَ ﴾ يوسف: ١٠٨

"Say: This is my way, I invite [people] to Allah upon insight, I and those who follow me. Exalted be Allah, and I am not from the polytheists."
[12:108]

15.2 VOCABULARY OF THE VERSE

أَدْعُو إِلَى اللهِ	هَذِهِ سَبِيلِي	قُلْ
وَسُبْحَانَ اللهِ	أَنَا وَمَنِ اتَّبَعَنِي	عَلَى بَصِيرَةٍ
		وَمَا أَنَا مِنَ المُشْرِكِينَ

15.3 AN ARABIC LANGUAGE BENEFIT

TIP: *Review module 6.3 on p.28.*

The word ما ("*maa*") can be used to negate a noun-based sentence. Consider how this occurs in this Verse and other Quranic passages, as summarized in the following table. Notice that sometimes a *baa'* is added as well. Complete the missing examples, and then add some more examples that you find in your reading to complete the table.

جُملَةٌ اسْمِيَّةٌ مَنْفِيَّةٌ بِـ"مَا"	جُملَةٌ اسْمِيَّةٌ مُثْبِتَةٌ
﴿وَمَا أَنَا مِنَ الْمُشْرِكِينَ﴾	وَأَنَا مِنَ الْمُشْرِكِينَ
﴿ ﴾ ص: ٨٦	وَأَنَا مِنَ الْمُتَكَلِّفِينَ
﴿ ﴾ القلم: ٢	أَنْتَ مَجْنُونٌ
﴿ ﴾ آل عمران: ٧٨	وَهُوَ مِنَ الْكِتَابِ
﴿ ﴾ آل عمران: ٧٨	وَهُوَ مِنْ عِنْدِ اللهِ
﴿ ﴾ التكوير: ٢٥	وَهُوَ قَوْلُ شَيْطَانٍ رَجِيمٍ

15.4 TAFSEER BENEFITS

TIP: *Review Lesson 7, pp.31-34.*

The Verse addresses whom?	
What is "this way"?	
Da'wah has a lofty focus	
Da'wah is not just speech	
"Those who follow me"	
Being a true follower	
The meaning of *'Subhaan Allah'*	
Exalting Allah, when?	General:
	Specific:
Denouncing polytheism	

Da'wah has fundamentals	16:125
Grounded knowledge is needed	
Ignorance harms & corrupts	
Da'wah is Inviting and warning	

15.5 HADEETH STUDY

عَنْ عَبْدِ اللهِ بْنِ مَسْعُودٍ رَضِيَ اللهُ عَنْهُ، قَالَ: خَطَّ لَنَا رَسُولُ اللهِ
صَلَّى اللهُ عَلَيْهِ وَسَلَّمَ خَطًّا، ثُمَّ قَالَ: «هَذَا سَبِيلُ اللهِ.» ثُمَّ خَطَّ
خُطُوطًا عَنْ يَمِينِهِ وَعَنْ شِمَالِهِ، ثُمَّ قَالَ: «هَذِهِ سُبُلٌ مُتَفَرِّقَةٌ،
عَلَى كُلِّ سَبِيلٍ مِنْهَا شَيْطَانٌ يَدْعُو إِلَيْهِ.» ثُمَّ قَرَأَ: ﴿وَأَنَّ هَذَا
صِرَاطِي مُسْتَقِيمًا فَاتَّبِعُوهُ وَلَا تَتَّبِعُوا السُّبُلَ فَتَفَرَّقَ بِكُمْ عَنْ سَبِيلِهِ﴾
[الأنعام: ١٥٣]. أَخْرَجَهُ أَحْمَدُ، وَحَسَّنَهُ الْأَلْبَانِيُّ.

On the authority of 'Abdullaah ibn Mas'ood (may Allah be pleased with him), who said: The Messenger of Allah (may Allah raise his rank and grant him peace) drew a line, and then said, **"This is the Path of Allah."** Then, he drew lines to its right and left, and then said, **"These are different paths, upon each one of them is a devil calling to it."** Then he recited: **"And this is my straight path, so follow it! And do not follow the [other] paths, lest they split you away from His path."** [6:153] *Musnad Ahmad*, authentic

15.6 BENEFITS OF THE HADEETH

'Abdullaah ibn Mas'ood	
He drew a single line	

Other lines are stray paths	
Singularity vs. multiplicity of paths	
Da'wah is invitations & warnings	
Some callers are devils	
Truth & falsehood are incompatible	
Teaching with visual aids	
Using Quranic textual proofs	

15.7 RESEARCH: The Prophet (may Allah raise his rank and grant him peace) foretold the splitting of the Ummah into 73 religious sects. List as many as you can name and briefly describe the nature of their deviation.

16.1 QURAN STUDY

﴿ وَمَا أَرْسَلْنَا مِن قَبْلِكَ إِلَّا رِجَالًا نُّوحِي إِلَيْهِمْ فَاسْأَلُوا أَهْلَ الذِّكْرِ إِن كُنتُمْ لَا تَعْلَمُونَ ۝ بِالْبَيِّنَاتِ وَالزُّبُرِ وَأَنزَلْنَا إِلَيْكَ الذِّكْرَ لِتُبَيِّنَ لِلنَّاسِ مَا نُزِّلَ إِلَيْهِمْ وَلَعَلَّهُمْ يَتَفَكَّرُونَ ۝ ﴾ النحل

"And We have sent before you none but men whom We sent Revelation to. So ask the people of knowledge if you do not know. [Those men were sent] with clear evidences and Books of Revelation. And We have sent down to you the Reminder, in order for your to clarify for the people what has been sent down to them, and in order for them to reflect." [16:43-44]

16.2 VOCABULARY OF THE VERSES

إِلَّا رِجَالًا	مِنْ قَبْلِكَ	وَمَا أَرْسَلْنَا
إِنْ كُنْتُمْ لَا تَعْلَمُونَ	فَاسْأَلُوا أَهْلَ الذِّكْرِ	نُوحِي إِلَيْهِمْ
وَأَنْزَلْنَا إِلَيْكَ الذِّكْرَ	وَالزُّبُرِ	بِالْبَيِّنَاتِ
وَلَعَلَّهُمْ يَتَفَكَّرُونَ	مَا نُزِّلَ إِلَيْهِمْ	لِتُبَيِّنَ لِلنَّاسِ

16.3 AN ARABIC LANGUAGE CHALLENGE

From the Verse, extract each of the following language items (as shown in the example):

﴿أَرْسَلْنَا﴾	فِعْلُ مَاضٍ
	اسْمٌ مُعَرَّفٌ بِـ"ال"
	فِعْلُ مُضَارِعٍ
	جَمْعُ مُؤَنَّثٍ سَالِمٍ
	حَرْفُ جَرٍّ وَمَجْرُورٌ
	اسْمٌ ظَاهِرٌ مُضَافٌ إِلَيْهِ
	فِعْلٌ مَبْنِيٌّ لِلْمَجْهُولِ
	جَمْعُ تَكْسِيرٍ
	فِعْلُ أَمْرٍ
	أَدَاةُ اسْتِثْنَاءٍ
	اسْمٌ مَعْطُوفٌ عَلَى مَجْرُورٍ

16.4 TAFSEER BENEFITS

Messengers had Revelation	
Who are *"Ahluth-Thikr"*	
"When/if you do not know"	
Clear evidences & divine Books	
The Quran is **THE** *"Thikr"*	
Prophetic mission summarized	

Intended impact of Revelation	
Quran connects us to scholars	
Modern misinterpretation	

16.5 HADEETH STUDY

عَنْ أَنَسٍ رَضِيَ اللهُ عَنْهُ: أَنَّ الْيَهُودَ كَانُوا إِذَا حَاضَتِ الْمَرْأَةُ فِيهِمْ لَمْ يُؤَاكِلُوهَا، وَلَمْ يُجَامِعُوهُنَّ فِي الْبُيُوتِ، فَسَأَلَ أَصْحَابُ النَّبِيِّ النَّبِيِّ صَلَّى اللهُ عَلَيْهِ وَسَلَّمَ، فَأَنْزَلَ اللهُ تَعَالَى: ﴿وَيَسْـَٔلُونَكَ عَنِ ٱلْمَحِيضِ قُلْ هُوَ أَذًى فَٱعْتَزِلُوا ٱلنِّسَآءَ فِي ٱلْمَحِيضِ﴾ [البقرة: ٢٢٢]، إِلَى آخِرِ الْآيَةِ، فَقَالَ رَسُولُ اللهِ صَلَّى اللهُ عَلَيْهِ وَسَلَّمَ: «اصْنَعُوا كُلَّ شَيْءٍ إِلَّا النِّكَاحَ.»

[أَخْرَجَهُ مُسْلِمٌ]

On the authority of Anas (may Allah be pleased with him), who said: When Jewish women menstruated, they (their husbands) would not eat together with them; they would not even stay in the same house with them. So some of the Companions asked the Prophet (may Allah raise his rank and grant him peace), and Allah, the Most High, revealed: **"And they ask you about menstruation. Say: It is harmful, so stay away from the women during menstruation..."** [2:222], to the end of the Verse. Then, the Messenger of Allah (may Allah raise his rank and grant him peace) said, **"Do everything except intercourse."** [Saheeh Muslim]

16.6 BENEFITS OF THE HADEETH

Anas	
Rigidity of Jewish regulations	
Returning things to the Prophet	

Answers came as revelation	
The complete Verse: 2:222	
The ambiguity of the wordings	
Intended meaning specified	By his speech:
	By his actions:
Connection to 16:44	
Review Lesson 15	
A core principle in Tafseer	

16.7 REVIEW: Look back at all the lessons of this workbook. By Allah's Permission, each lesson illustrates at least one angle of how the Sunnah provides detailed explanations for Quranic passages. Summarize those relationships in five of your favorite lessons.

SCALES OF JUSTICE ON THE DAY OF JUDGMENT

17.1 QURAN STUDY

وَنَضَعُ ٱلْمَوَازِينَ ٱلْقِسْطَ لِيَوْمِ ٱلْقِيَامَةِ فَلَا تُظْلَمُ نَفْسٌ شَيْئًا وَإِن كَانَ مِثْقَالَ حَبَّةٍ مِّنْ خَرْدَلٍ أَتَيْنَا بِهَا وَكَفَىٰ بِنَا حَاسِبِينَ ﴾ الأنبياء: ٤٧

"And We shall set in place the Scales of Justice for the Day of Resurrection, so no soul shall be wronged in the slightest way. Even if it were just the weight of a mustard seed, We shall bring it. And sufficient are We to take account." [21:47]

17.2 VOCABULARY OF THE VERSE

وَنَضَعُ	الْمَوَازِينَ	الْقِسْطَ
لِيَوْمِ الْقِيَامَةِ	فَلَا تُظْلَمُ نَفْسٌ شَيْئًا	وَإِنْ كَانَ مِثْقَالَ حَبَّةٍ
مِنْ خَرْدَلٍ	أَتَيْنَا بِهَا	وَكَفَى بِنَا حَاسِبِينَ

17.3 AN ARABIC LANGUAGE BENEFIT

In the science of *Sarf* (Morphology), linguists categorize all letters into either صحيح ("*saheeh*", like our consonants) or حرف علة ("*harf 'illah*", similar to our vowels). All the letters of the alphabet are *saheeh*, except for three *harf 'illah* letters: ا – و - ي. Built upon this, all verbs are then categorized as *saheeh* or *mu'tall*. Saheeh verbs have no *harf 'illah*, and *mu'tall* verbs have at least one *harf 'illah*. Consider how the verbs in the Verse are either *saheeh* or *mu'tall* and why in the following table. Add two more verbs yourself.

71

السبب	معتل	صحيح	الفعل
فِيهِ حَرْفُ الوَاوِ	✔		وَضَعَ
لَا حَرْفَ عِلَّةٍ فِيهِ		✔	ظَلَمَ
	✔		كَانَ
			كَفَى
			أَتَى
			حَسِبَ
	✔		
		✔	

Note: The letter *"hamzah"* is considered *saheeh*, not a *harf 'illah*.

17.4 TAFSEER BENEFITS

The placing of the Scales		
Real scales Vs. *Mu'tazilah* belief		
What is weighed on them?	1	
	2	
	3	
	4	
The weight of a mustard seed		
The benefit of this weighing		

17.5 HADEETH STUDY

عَنْ أَبِي هُرَيْرَةَ رَضِيَ اللهُ عَنْهُ، عَنِ النَّبِيِّ صَلَّى اللهُ عَلَيْهِ وَسَلَّمَ، قَالَ:

«كَلِمَتَانِ خَفِيفَتَانِ عَلَى اللِّسَانِ، ثَقِيلَتَانِ فِي الْمِيزَانِ، حَبِيبَتَانِ إِلَى

الرَّحْمَنِ: سُبْحَانَ اللهِ وَبِحَمْدِهِ، سُبْحَانَ اللهِ الْعَظِيمِ.» [مُتَّفَقٌ عَلَيْهِ]

On the authority of Aboo Hurayrah, from the Prophet (may Allah raise his rank and grant him peace), who said: "Two phrases are light on the tongue, yet heavy in the Scale and beloved to the Most Merciful: Exalted be Allah, and the Praise is for him; exalted be Allah, the Great."
[Agreed upon]

17.6 BENEFITS OF THE HADEETH

Two "kalimahs"	
Light on the tongue	
Heavy on the Scale	
Love as a Divine Attribute	
The indication in "ar-Rahmaan"	
Exalting Allah: "Subhaan Allah"	Specific
	General
Praise is due to Allah	
Allah's Name: "al-'Atheem"	
Last hadeeth of al-Bukhaaree	

17.7 ACTIVITY: Memorize the supplication from 17.5, and use it throughout your day and night. Memorize the entire wording of the hadeeth too, and share it with others.

«كَلِمَتَانِ خَفِيفَتَانِ عَلَى اللِّسَانِ،

ثَقِيلَتَانِ فِي الْمِيزَانِ، حَبِيبَتَانِ إِلَى الرَّحْمنِ:

سُبْحَانَ اللهِ وَبِحَمْدِهِ، سُبْحَانَ اللهِ الْعَظِيمِ.»

18.1 QURAN STUDY

﴿ إِنَّ الَّذِينَ يُحِبُّونَ أَن تَشِيعَ الْفَاحِشَةُ فِي الَّذِينَ ءَامَنُوا لَهُمْ عَذَابٌ أَلِيمٌ فِي الدُّنْيَا وَالْآخِرَةِ وَاللَّهُ يَعْلَمُ وَأَنتُمْ لَا تَعْلَمُونَ ﴾ النور: ١٩

"Verily, those who love that allegations of illicit behavior be spread about those who believe shall have a painful punishment in this life and the Next. And Allah knows, while you know not." [24:19]

18.2 VOCABULARY OF THE VERSE

فِي الَّذِينَ آمَنُوا	أَنْ تَشِيعَ الفَاحِشَةُ	إِنَّ الَّذِينَ يُحِبُّونَ
وَالآخِرَةِ	فِي الدُّنْيَا	لَهُمْ عَذَابٌ أَلِيمٌ
	وَأَنْتُمْ لَا تَعْلَمُونَ	وَاللهُ يَعْلَمُ

18.3 AN ARABIC LANGUAGE BENEFIT

Nouns have adjectives in Arabic, but the order of the two words is the opposite of what we are used to in English. In English we say, "a painful punishment," with the adjective before the noun. Think about how "punishment" is described as "painful" in the Verse we have just studied. Also, consider the other examples in the following table, and complete the missing fields.

الصفة	الاسم	الآية
أَلِيمٌ	عَذَابٌ	﴿ لَهُمۡ عَذَابٌ أَلِيمٌ ﴾ النور: ١٩
		﴿ إِلَّا فِي كِتَٰبٍ مُّبِينٍ ﴾ يونس: ٦١
		﴿ ذَٰلِكَ ٱلدِّينُ ٱلۡقَيِّمُ ﴾ التوبة: ٣٦
		﴿ وَٱللَّهُ ذُو ٱلۡفَضۡلِ ٱلۡعَظِيمِ ﴾ الأنفال: ٢٩
		﴿ مِنۡهُ ءَايَٰتٌ مُّحۡكَمَٰتٌ ﴾ آل عمران: ٧
		﴿ حَتَّىٰ يَتَبَيَّنَ لَكُمُ ٱلۡخَيۡطُ ٱلۡأَبۡيَضُ ﴾ البقرة: ١٨٧
		﴿ مِنَ ٱلۡخَيۡطِ ٱلۡأَسۡوَدِ مِنَ ٱلۡفَجۡرِ ﴾ البقرة: ١٨٧

18.4 TAFSEER BENEFITS

Merely enjoying rumors		
Punishment in this life		
Punishment in the Hereafter		
Allegations without witnesses: Legal ramifications (24:4)	1	
	2	
	3	
Further ramifications (24:23-24)	1	
	2	
	3	
Allah's Knowledge		
Our ignorance		

18.5 HADEETH STUDY

عَنِ ابْنِ عُمَرَ رَضِيَ اللهُ عَنْهُمَا، قَالَ: صَعِدَ رَسُولُ اللهِ صَلَّى اللهُ عَلَيْهِ وَسَلَّمَ الْمِنْبَرَ، فَنَادَى بِصَوْتٍ رَفِيعٍ، فَقَالَ: «يَا مَعْشَرَ مَنْ أَسْلَمَ بِلِسَانِهِ وَلَمْ يُفْضِ الْإِيمَانُ إِلَى قَلْبِهِ! لاَ تُؤْذُوا الْمُسْلِمِينَ! وَلاَ تُعَيِّرُوهُمْ! وَلاَ تَتَّبَّعُوا عَوْرَاتِهِمْ، فَإِنَّهُ مَنْ تَتَبَّعَ عَوْرَةَ أَخِيهِ الْمُسْلِمِ تَتَبَّعَ اللهُ عَوْرَتَهُ، وَمَنْ تَتَبَّعَ اللهُ عَوْرَتَهُ يَفْضَحْهُ وَلَوْ فِي جَوْفِ رَحْلِهِ!» [أَخْرَجَهُ التِّرْمِذِيُّ، وَقَالَ حَسَنٌ غَرِيبٌ، وَصَحَّحَهُ الْأَلْبَانِيُّ]

On the authority of Ibn 'Umar (may Allah be pleased with him and his father), who said: The Messenger of Allah (may Allah raise his rank and grant him peace), ascended the *minbar* and called out with a loud voice, saying: **"O gathering of those who have only accepted Islam upon their tongues while faith has not yet entered their hearts! Do not harm the Muslims! Do not criticize them, and do not seek out their hidden faults! Certainly, whoever seeks out the hidden faults of his Muslim brother, Allah shall expose his hidden faults. And if Allah exposes the hidden faults of a person, He disgraces him, even within the depths of his own home!"** [*At-Tirmithee*, authentic]

18.6 BENEFITS OF THE HADEETH

Ibn 'Umar	
Raised voice, from the *minbar*	
Muslims without *eemaan*?	
The three prohibitions:	1
	2
	3

Special focus on the third one	
Punishment matches crime	
The opposite understanding	
Criticism is legislated in limited scenarios:	1
	2
	3
	4
	5
	6
Criticizing the above critics	
Internet anonymity	
Blessings misused = ingratitude	

18.7 CONTEMPLATION AND DISCUSSION: Consider the possible motives that some people may have for spreading accusations of Muslims anonymously on the internet.

19.1 QURAN STUDY

وَمِنَ ٱلنَّاسِ مَن يَقُولُ ءَامَنَّا بِٱللَّهِ فَإِذَآ أُوذِىَ فِى ٱللَّهِ جَعَلَ فِتْنَةَ ٱلنَّاسِ كَعَذَابِ ٱللَّهِ وَلَئِن جَآءَ نَصْرٌ مِّن رَّبِّكَ لَيَقُولُنَّ إِنَّا كُنَّا مَعَكُمْ أَوَلَيْسَ ٱللَّهُ بِأَعْلَمَ بِمَا فِى صُدُورِ ٱلْعَالَمِينَ ﴿ العنكبوت: ١٠

"Among the people is he who says, 'I have believed in Allah,' yet when he is harmed in the way of Allah, he considers the people's calamities like the Punishment of Allah. Had some victory come from your Lord, they would surely be saying: 'We have always been with you!' Isn't Allah most knowledgeable of what is in the chests of all the creation?"
[29:10]

19.2 VOCABULARY OF THE VERSE

كَعَذَابِ الله	جَعَلَ فِتْنَةَ النَّاسِ	فَإِذَا أُوذِيَ فِي الله
إِنَّا كُنَّا مَعَكُمْ	لَيَقُولُنَّ	نَصْرٌ مِنْ رَبِّكَ
	بِمَا فِي صُدُورِ العَالَمِينَ	أَوَلَيْسَ اللهُ بِأَعْلَمَ

19.3 AN ARABIC LANGUAGE BENEFIT

When two nouns come consecutively in the Arabic Language, and they are considered *mudhaaf* and *mudhaaf ilayhe*, it means that the first noun is "of" or related to the second noun, sometimes the owned property, and sometimes another kind of relativity. The Arabic phrase, رسول الله "Rasool Allah", means: the rasool (Messenger) "of" Allah. This kind of "idhaafah" construction is found three times in the Verse we have just studied. Consider how the two nouns are constructed in each instance, as represented in the following table, as well as in the other examples. Try to fill in the missing fields as much as you can, and then add another example that you find yourself.

المضاف إليه	المضاف	الآية
النَّاسِ	فِتْنَةَ	﴿جَعَلَ فِتْنَةَ النَّاسِ كَعَذَابِ اللَّهِ﴾ العنكبوت: ١٠
اللهِ	عَذَابِ	﴿جَعَلَ فِتْنَةَ النَّاسِ كَعَذَابِ اللَّهِ﴾ العنكبوت: ١٠
العَالَمِينَ	صُدُورِ	﴿بِمَا فِي صُدُورِ الْعَالَمِينَ﴾ العنكبوت: ١٠
	يَوْم	﴿وَنَضَعُ الْمَوَازِينَ الْقِسْطَ لِيَوْمِ الْقِيَامَةِ﴾ الأنبياء: ٤٧
		﴿وَإِن كَانَ مِثْقَالَ حَبَّةٍ مِّنْ خَرْدَلٍ﴾ الأنبياء: ٤٧
	أَهْلَ	﴿فَسْـَٔلُوا﴾ الأنبياء: ٧
		﴿ ﴾ الأنعام: ١٦٥

19.4 TAFSEER BENEFITS

From among the people	
They say a good word openly	
They keep evil concealed	
How hypocrites view trials	
Yet in time of prosperity	

Contradictions of hypocrites	Speech/action
	Inner/outer
Returning to the All-Knowing	
He knows what the chests hide	

19.5 HADEETH STUDY

عَنْ عَبْدِ اللهِ بْنِ عَمْرٍو رَضِيَ اللهُ عَنْهُمَا، قَالَ: قَالَ رَسُولُ اللهِ صَلَّى اللهُ عَلَيْهِ وَسَلَّمَ: ﴿أَرْبَعٌ مَنْ كُنَّ فِيهِ كَانَ مُنَافِقًا خَالِصًا، وَمَنْ كَانَتْ فِيهِ خَصْلَةٌ مِنْهُنَّ كَانَتْ فِيهِ خَصْلَةٌ مِنْ نِفَاقٍ حَتَّى يَدَعَهَا: إِذَا حَدَّثَ كَذَبَ، وَإِذَا عَاهَدَ غَدَرَ، وَإِذَا وَعَدَ أَخْلَفَ، وَإِذَا خَاصَمَ فَجَرَ﴾

[مُتَّفَقٌ عَلَيْهِ]

On the authority of 'Abdullaah ibn 'Amr (may Allah be pleased with him and his father), the Messenger of Allah (may Allah raise his rank and grant him peace) said: **"When four things are found in a person, he is a true hypocrite; and whoever has one of them has a trait of hypocrisy until he abandons it: [1] When he speaks, he lies. [2] When he enters an agreement, he betrays it. [3] When he makes a promise, he breaks it. [4] When he argues, he behaves wickedly."** [Agreed upon]

19.6 BENEFITS OF THE HADEETH

'Abdullaah ibn 'Amr	
Hypocrisy is two basic types:	1
	2
A "true" hypocrite in this text	

Four traits of hypocrisy:	1	
	2	
	3	
	4	
Feeling safe from hypocrisy		

19.7 RESEARCH: Compile a list of the traits of the hypocrites from the Quran. Here are a few Verses to get you started:

2:8	They claim to believe in Allah & Last Day, but they do not
2:9	They are deceptive, only deceiving themselves & don't realize
2:10	Diseased hearts, getting worse, they lie
2:11	They do not accept advice, while they claim righteousness
2:12	They are mischief makers & don't realize
2:13	
2:14	
2:15	
2:16	
2:17	
2:18	
2:19	
2:20	

20.1 QURAN STUDY

مَا كَانَ مُحَمَّدٌ أَبَا أَحَدٍ مِّن رِّجَالِكُمْ وَلَٰكِن رَّسُولَ ٱللَّهِ وَخَاتَمَ ٱلنَّبِيِّنَ ۗ وَكَانَ ٱللَّهُ بِكُلِّ شَيْءٍ عَلِيمًا ۝ الأحزاب: ٤٠

"Muhammad is not the father of any of your men. However, he is the Messenger of Allah and the seal of the Prophets. And Allah is, regarding all things, All-Knowing." [33:40]

20.2 VOCABULARY OF THE VERSE

وَلَٰكِنْ رَسُولَ الله	أَبَا أَحَدٍ مِنْ رِجَالِكُمْ	مَا كَانَ مُحَمَّدٌ
بِكُلِّ شَيْءٍ عَلِيمًا	وَكَانَ اللهُ	وَخَاتَمَ النَّبِيِّينَ

20.3 AN ARABIC LANGUAGE BENEFIT

The verb كَانَ (kaana) comes with two nouns: its subject (اسم كان) and its predicate (خبر كان). Its subject is *marfoo'*, and its object is *mansoob*. Look at two examples in the Verse:

خبر كان [منصوب]	اسم كان [مرفوع]
﴿أَبَا أَحَدٍ مِّن رِّجَالِكُمْ﴾	﴿مَا كَانَ مُحَمَّدٌ﴾
﴿بِكُلِّ شَيْءٍ عَلِيمًا﴾	﴿وَكَانَ ٱللَّهُ﴾

In the following table, consider how the structures of the sentences change, when *kaana* is absent (on the right), and when *kaana* is used (on the left). Try to complete the table:

﴿ وَكَانَ ٱللَّهُ بِكُلِّ شَيْءٍ عَلِيمًا ﴾	وَٱللَّهُ بِكُلِّ شَيْءٍ عَلِيمٌ
﴿ وَكَانَ سَعْيُكُم مَّشْكُورًا ﴾ الإنسان: ٢٢	وَسَعْيُكُمْ مَشْكُورٌ
الفتح: ٢٤ ﴿ ﴾	وَٱللَّهُ بِمَا تَعْمَلُونَ بَصِيرٌ
﴿ وَكَانَ ٱللَّهُ عَزِيزًا حَكِيمًا ﴾ الفتح: ١٩	
الأحزاب: ٥٢ ﴿ ﴾	وَٱللَّهُ عَلَىٰ كُلِّ شَيْءٍ رَقِيبٌ

20.4 TAFSEER BENEFITS

A negation of fatherhood		
An implied kind of fatherhood		
Prophet's name without title		
Messengership affirmed		
Definition of a Messenger		
Definition of a Prophet		
Definition of a *khaatam* (seal)		
The Name *'Aleem* refers to:	1	
	2	
	3	
Islamic ruling on false prophets		

20.5 HADEETH STUDY

عَنْ أَبِي هُرَيْرَةَ رَضِيَ اللهُ عَنْهُ: أَنَّ رَسُولَ اللهِ صَلَّى اللهُ عَلَيْهِ وَسَلَّمَ قَالَ:

«مَثَلِي وَمَثَلُ الْأَنْبِيَاءِ مِنْ قَبْلِي، كَمَثَلِ رَجُلٍ بَنَى بَيْتًا، فَأَحْسَنَهُ

وَأَجْمَلَهُ، إِلَّا مَوْضِعَ لَبِنَةٍ مِنْ زَاوِيَةٍ، فَجَعَلَ النَّاسُ يَطُوفُونَ بِهِ،

وَيَعْجَبُونَ لَهُ، وَيَقُولُونَ: هَلَّا وُضِعَتْ هَذِهِ اللَّبِنَةُ؟ فَأَنَا اللَّبِنَةُ، وَأَنَا

خَاتَمُ النَّبِيِّينَ» [مُتَّفَقٌ عَلَيْهِ]

On the authority of Aboo Hurayrah (may Allah raise his rank and grant him peace): The Messenger of Allah (may Allah raise his rank and grant him peace) said: **"My likeness as it relates to the Prophets before me is like how a man builds a house, he builds it well and decorates it beautifully, with the exception of one missing brick on one corner. So the people take to circling about the house, admiring it, saying: 'If only this last brick could be added in!' And I am that brick; I am the seal of the Prophets."** [Agreed upon]

20.6 BENEFITS OF THE HADEETH

Aboo Hurayrah	
Prophetic parables	
One single missing brick	
Singularity & finality stressed	
Examples of false prophets	1
	2
	3
	4

20.7 HISTORICAL RESEARCH: The Prophet (may Allah raise his rank and grant him peace) foretold the coming of thirty false prophets. How many of them can you name? Begin with the examples you've heard in today's lesson, and add as many as you can find information about:

#	Name	Time/place	About him/her
1	Musaylimah b. Habeeb	1st century Arabia	Killed in Battle of Yamaamah, year 12

THE DUTY OF DISCHARGING ZAKAAT AL-FITR

21.1 QURAN STUDY

﴿ وَإِذَا قِيلَ لَهُمْ أَنفِقُوا مِمَّا رَزَقَكُمُ اللَّهُ قَالَ الَّذِينَ كَفَرُوا لِلَّذِينَ ءَامَنُوا أَنُطْعِمُ مَن لَّوْ
يَشَاءُ اللَّهُ أَطْعَمَهُ إِنْ أَنتُمْ إِلَّا فِي ضَلَالٍ مُّبِينٍ ﴾ يس : ٤٧

"And when it is said to them: 'Spend from what Allah has provided you with,' Those who disbelieve say to those who believe: 'Are we going to feed those whom Allah would have already fed if He wanted? You are but in clear misguidance!'" [36:47]

21.2 VOCABULARY OF THE VERSE

مِمَّا رَزَقَكُمُ اللهُ	أَنْفِقُوا	وَإِذَا قِيلَ لَهُمْ
أَنُطْعِمُ مَنْ	لِلَّذِينَ آمَنُوا	قَالَ الَّذِينَ كَفَرُوا
فِي ضَلَالٍ مُبِينٍ	إِنْ أَنْتُمْ إِلَّا	لَوْ شَاءَ اللهُ لَأَطْعَمَهُ

21.3 AN ARABIC LANGUAGE BENEFIT

Adding a *hamzah* to the beginning of some past-tense verbs makes the verb transitive. The best way to explain this is through examples. Think about how this operation changes the meanings of the following verbs, and then try to complete the table.

أَطْعَمَ He made someone eat	طَعِمَ He ate
أَضَلَّ He made someone go astray	ضَلَّ He went astray
أَخْرَجَ He made someone leave	خَرَجَ He left
	دَخَلَ He entered
أَقَامَ He made someone stand	
	He read

21.4 TAFSEER BENEFITS

When it is said to "them"	
Spending is a kind of worship	
All provisions are from Allah	
Qadr and passivism	
Calling the believers misguided	
False speech worded strongly	

21.5 HADEETH STUDY

عَنِ ابْنِ عُمَرَ رَضِيَ اللَّهُ عَنْهُمَا، قَالَ: فَرَضَ رَسُولُ اللَّهِ صَلَّى اللَّهُ عَلَيْهِ وَسَلَّمَ زَكَاةَ الْفِطْرِ صَاعًا مِنْ تَمْرٍ، أَوْ صَاعًا مِنْ شَعِيرٍ، عَلَى الْعَبْدِ وَالْحُرِّ، وَالذَّكَرِ وَالْأُنْثَى، وَالصَّغِيرِ وَالْكَبِيرِ مِنَ الْمُسْلِمِينَ، وَأَمَرَ بِهَا أَنْ تُؤَدَّى قَبْلَ خُرُوجِ النَّاسِ إِلَى الصَّلَاةِ. [مُتَّفَقٌ عَلَيْهِ]

On the authority of Ibn 'Umar (may Allah be pleased with him and his father), who said: "The Messenger of Allah (may Allah raise his rank and grant him peace) obligated *Zakaat al-Fitr* as a *saa'* of dates or a *saa'* of barley upon every Muslim, free or captive, male or female, young or old. He ordered that it be given out before the people go out for the prayer."
[Agreed upon]

21.6 BENEFITS OF THE HADEETH

Ibn 'Umar	
Zakaat al-Fitr is an obligation	
The size of a *saa'* container	
Dates or barley (only?)	
Who is it given to?	
Can we give money instead?	
When must it be given?	
Why you should give it out yourself (and not deputize others without need):	1
	2
	3
	4

21.7 RESEARCH: Use a *saa'* container or standard measuring cups or pitchers to measure out three liters of three or more different kinds of staple food. Weigh the *saa'* of each kind of food and record the weights in the table below. You should be able to make an important conclusion about the relationship between weight and volume as it relates to how food is given for *Zakaat al-Fitr, in shaa' Allah*.

Staple food	Weight of 3L (1 Saa')

22.1 QURAN STUDY

بِسْمِ حمٓ ۝ وَٱلْكِتَٰبِ ٱلْمُبِينِ ۝ إِنَّآ أَنزَلْنَٰهُ فِى لَيْلَةٍ مُّبَٰرَكَةٍ إِنَّا كُنَّا مُنذِرِينَ ۝ فِيهَا يُفْرَقُ كُلُّ أَمْرٍ حَكِيمٍ ۝ أَمْرًا مِّنْ عِندِنَآ إِنَّا كُنَّا مُرْسِلِينَ ۝ رَحْمَةً مِّن رَّبِّكَ إِنَّهُ هُوَ ٱلسَّمِيعُ ٱلْعَلِيمُ ۝ رَبِّ ٱلسَّمَٰوَٰتِ وَٱلْأَرْضِ وَمَا بَيْنَهُمَآ إِن كُنتُم مُّوقِنِينَ ۝ لَآ إِلَٰهَ إِلَّا هُوَ يُحْىِۦ وَيُمِيتُ رَبُّكُمْ وَرَبُّ ءَابَآئِكُمُ ٱلْأَوَّلِينَ ۝ الدخان

"*Haa-Meem*. By the Clear Book. Verily, We have sent it down in a blessed night. Verily, We have always been ever-warning. Therein, every wise order is set. An order, from Us. Verily, We are ever-sending (Messengers, decrees, etc.). Mercy, from your Lord. Verily, He is the All-Hearing, the All-Knowing. The Lord of the heavens and the earth and all that is between them, if you only knew for certain. There is no one worthy of worship other than Him. He gives life and causes death, your Lord and the Lord of your forefathers of old." [44:1-8]

22.2 VOCABULARY OF THE VERSES

فِي لَيْلَةٍ مُبَارَكَةٍ	إِنَّا أَنْزَلْنَاهُ	وَالْكِتَابِ الْمُبِينِ
أَمْرًا مِنْ عِنْدِنَا	كُلُّ أَمْرٍ حَكِيمٍ	فِيهَا يُفْرَقُ
يُحْيِي وَيُمِيتُ	السَّمِيعُ الْعَلِيمُ	رَحْمَةً مِنْ رَبِّكَ

22.3 AN ARABIC LANGUAGE BENEFIT

Think about how Allah did not simply say: نَحن منذرون (We are ever-warning), but rather devices of emphasis are used to say: إنا كنا منذرين (Verily We have always been ever-warning). The same style of emphasis is used another time in the same Verse. Try to follow the same pattern and predict what the other three Verses say in the following table:

﴿ إِنَّا كُنَّا مُنْذِرِينَ ﴾ الدخان: ٣	نَحْنُ مُنْذِرُونَ
﴿ إِنَّا كُنَّا مُرْسِلِينَ ﴾ الدخان: ٥	نَحْنُ مُرْسِلُونَ
﴿ ﴾ الأنبياء: ١٠٤	نَحْنُ فَاعِلُونَ
﴿ ﴾ الأعراف: ٥	نَحْنُ ظَالِمُونَ
﴿ ﴾ الأعراف: ١٧٢	نَحْنُ عَنْ هذَا غَافِلُونَ

22.4 TAFSEER BENEFITS

Letters that start some *soorahs*		
Allah swears by His Book		
The Revelation of the Quran	In one night:	
	Over 23 years:	
A blessed night: *Laylat al-Qadr*		
Allah issues warnings		
All wise orders are set		
Allaah is ever-sending… (what)		
As Mercy from Allah		
Allah is the All-Hearing		
Allah is the All-Knowing		
His unchallenged Lordship		

Testimony of *towheed*	
He brings life, causes death	
Lord of all people, past & present	

22.5 HADEETH STUDY

عَنْ عَائِشَةَ رَضِيَ اللهُ عَنْهَا: أَنَّ رَسُولَ اللهِ صَلَّى اللهُ عَلَيْهِ وَسَلَّمَ، قَالَ: «تَحَرَّوْا لَيْلَةَ القَدْرِ فِي الوِتْرِ مِنَ العَشْرِ الأَوَاخِرِ مِنْ رَمَضَانَ» [مُتَّفَقٌ عَلَيْهِ]

On the authority of 'Aa'ishah (may Allah be pleased with her): The Messenger of Allah (may Allah raise his rank and grant him peace) said: **"Seek out *Laylat al-Qadr* (the Night of Decree) in the odd [nights] of the last ten [nights] of Ramadhaan."** [Agreed upon]

22.6 BENEFITS OF THE HADEETH

'Aa'ishah	
Laylat al-Qadr is sought out	
Odd nights of the last ten	
How to seek it out	

22.7 ACTIVITY: Memorize the supplication found in an authentic hadeeth collected by Imaam at-Tirmithee and others, when 'Aa'ishah asked what she should say if she caught *Laytal-Qadr*. The Prophet (may Allah raise his rank and grant him peace) instructed her to supplicate:

«اللّهُمَّ إِنَّكَ عَفُوٌّ، تُحِبُّ الْعَفْوَ، فَاعْفُ عَنِّي!»

"O Allah! Certainly, You are the One who pardons;
You love to pardon, so pardon me!"

UNWARRANTED SUSPICION & BACKBITING

23.1 QURAN STUDY

يَٰٓأَيُّهَا ٱلَّذِينَ ءَامَنُوا۟ ٱجْتَنِبُوا۟ كَثِيرًا مِّنَ ٱلظَّنِّ إِنَّ بَعْضَ ٱلظَّنِّ إِثْمٌ وَلَا تَجَسَّسُوا۟ وَلَا يَغْتَب بَّعْضُكُم بَعْضًا أَيُحِبُّ أَحَدُكُمْ أَن يَأْكُلَ لَحْمَ أَخِيهِ مَيْتًا فَكَرِهْتُمُوهُ وَٱتَّقُوا۟ ٱللَّهَ إِنَّ ٱللَّهَ تَوَّابٌ رَّحِيمٌ ١٢ :الحجرات

"O you who have believed! Shun much suspicion, as some kinds of suspicion are sinful. Do not spy, and do backbite one another. Would any of you like to eat the flesh of his dead brother? You would hate it, so fear Allah! Verily, Allah is Ever-Accepting of repentance, Ever-Merciful." [49:12]

23.2 VOCABULARY OF THE VERSE

إِنَّ بَعْضَ الظَّنِّ إِثْمٌ	كَثِيرًا مِنَ الظَّنِّ	اجْتَنِبُوا
بَعْضُكُم بَعْضًا	وَلَا يَغْتَب	وَلَا تَجَسَّسُوا
لَحْمَ أَخِيهِ	أَنْ يَأْكُلَ	أَيُحِبُّ أَحَدُكُمْ
تَوَّابٌ	فَكَرِهْتُمُوهُ	مَيْتًا

23.3 AN ARABIC LANGUAGE CHALLENGE

TIP: *Review 16.3, our previous "challenge".*

From the Verse, try to extract each of the following language items (as shown in the example). Find the one request which cannot be fulfilled from the language of this Verse.

	﴿يَأْكُلَ﴾	فِعْلٌ مُضَارِعٍ
		اسْمٌ مُعَرَّفٌ بِـ"ال"
		فِعْلٌ مَاضٍ
		هَمْزَةُ الِاسْتِفْهَامِ
		حَرْفُ جَرٍّ وَمَجْرُورٌ
		مُضَافٌ وَمُضَافٌ إِلَيْهِ
		خَبَرُ إِنَّ
		جَمْعُ تَكْسِيرٍ
		فِعْلُ أَمْرٍ
		اسْمُ إِنَّ
		حَرْفُ نِدَاءٍ

23.4 TAFSEER BENEFITS

The call: "O you who believe…"	
Shunning suspicion	
"Some" suspicion is sinful	
The implied understanding	
Prohibition of spying	
Supervisory roles vs. spying	
Prohibition of backbiting	
When is backbiting allowed? *(Review your notes from 18.6)*	1
	2
	3
	4
	5
	6
Victim of backbiting (parable)	
Allah is *"Tawwaab"*	
Allah is Ever-Merciful	
Implied in the end of the Verse	

23.5 HADEETH STUDY

عَنْ أَبِي هُرَيْرَةَ رَضِيَ اللهُ عَنْهُ، عَنِ النَّبِيِّ صَلَّى اللهُ عَلَيْهِ وَسَلَّمَ، قَالَ:
«إِيَّاكُمْ وَالظَّنَّ، فَإِنَّ الظَّنَّ أَكْذَبُ الْحَدِيثِ، وَلَا تَحَسَّسُوا، وَلَا
تَجَسَّسُوا، وَلَا تَحَاسَدُوا، وَلَا تَدَابَرُوا، وَلاَ تَبَاغَضُوا، وَكُونُوا عِبَادَ
اللهِ إِخْوَانًا!» [مُتَّفَقٌ عَلَيْهِ]

On the authority of Aboo Hurayrah (may Allah be pleased with him), from the Prophet (may Allah raise his rank and grant him peace), who said: **"Be warned of suspicion, for verily suspicion is the most false kind of speech. Do not eavesdrop and do not spy. Do not envy one another. Do not turn your backs on one another. Do not hate one another. But be, O servants of Allah, brothers!"** [Agreed upon]

23.6 BENEFITS OF THE HADEETH

Aboo Hurayrah	
A warning against suspicion	
Suspicion is false speech	
Prohibitions	"tahas-sus"
	"tajas-sus"
	jealousy
	turning away
	hating Muslims
The order to be brothers	
A principle in interactions	
Consequences of misapplying it	

98

23.7 ACTIVITY: Summarize the upright manners and morals as found in the brief chapter, *Soorah al-Hujuraat*. Identify those you feel you are not implementing well enough, and set up a clear and practical plan to improve that behavior.

49:1	
49:2	
49:3	
49:4	
49:5	
49:6	
49:7	
49:8	
49:9	
49:10	
49:11	
49:12	
49:13	
49:14	
49:15	
49:16	
49:17	
49:18	

LESSON 24

AVOIDING MAJOR SINS & SEXUAL MISCONDUCT

24.1 QURAN STUDY

﴿ ٱلَّذِينَ يَجْتَنِبُونَ كَبَائِرَ ٱلْإِثْمِ وَٱلْفَوَاحِشَ إِلَّا ٱللَّمَمَ إِنَّ رَبَّكَ وَاسِعُ ٱلْمَغْفِرَةِ هُوَ أَعْلَمُ بِكُمْ إِذْ أَنشَأَكُم مِّنَ ٱلْأَرْضِ وَإِذْ أَنتُمْ أَجِنَّةٌ فِي بُطُونِ أُمَّهَاتِكُمْ فَلَا تُزَكُّوٓا أَنفُسَكُمْ هُوَ أَعْلَمُ بِمَنِ ٱتَّقَىٰ ﴾ النجم: ٣٢

"Those who avoid major sins and sexual misconduct, except for small errors. Verily, your Lord is abundantly forgiving. And He is most knowledgeable about you, as He made you from the earth, and then you were fetuses in the wombs of your mothers, so do not ascribe purity to yourselves. He is most knowledgeable about those who are pious." [53:32]

24.2 VOCABULARY OF THE VERSE

اللَّمَمَ	كَبَائِرَ الإِثْمِ	يَجْتَنِبُونَ
أَنْشَأَكُمْ مِنَ الأَرْضِ	هُوَ أَعْلَمُ بِكُمْ	وَاسِعُ المَغْفِرَةِ
فَلَا تُزَكُّوا أَنْفُسَكُمْ	فِي بُطُونِ أُمَّهَاتِكُمْ	أَجِنَّةٌ

101

24.3 AN ARABIC LANGUAGE BENEFIT

We can explain descriptions by making them relative to other things. A man being knowledgeable is a clear idea, however when a man is described as being more knowledgeable than a well-known knowledgeable figure, then the intended description becomes more clearly understood. Saying "Allah knows best" clarifies absolute superiority in that Attribute, in this case: complete and divinely perfect knowledge. Consider how a description in Arabic changes into the comparative form (أَفْعَلُ مِنْهُ), and then into the superlative form (أَفْعَلُ), in the table below, and then try to complete the missing language items:

Superlative	Comparative	Description
اللهُ أَعْلَمُ.	خَالِدٌ أَعْلَمُ مِنْ زَيْدٍ.	زَيْدٌ عَالِمٌ.
اللهُ أَكْبَرُ.	أَبُوهُ أَكْبَرُ مِنْهُ.	عَمْرٌو كَبِيرُ الشَّأْنِ.
أَحْمَدُ أَطْوَلُ الأَوْلَادِ.		رَشِيدٌ طَوِيلٌ.
	طَارِقٌ أَسْرَعُ مِنْ عُبَيْدٍ.	
		أَبُوكَ رَحِيمٌ.

24.4 TAFSEER BENEFITS

Context: *Sibaaq* & *lihaaq*	53:31
Avoiding major sins	
Definition of a major sin	
Definition of a minor sin	
Allah's expansive Forgiveness	
Allah's Knowledge	
People created from the earth	
Embryology in the Quran	22:5
	23:14

Prohibition of claiming purity	
The obligation of humility	
Allah knows about our piety	

24.5 HADEETH STUDY

عَنْ أَنَسِ بْنِ مَالِكٍ رَضِيَ اللهُ عَنْهُ، قَالَ: سُئِلَ رَسُولُ اللهِ صَلَّى اللهُ عَلَيْهِ وَسَلَّمَ عَنِ الكَبَائِرِ، فَقَالَ: «الشِّرْكُ بِاللهِ، وَقَتْلُ النَّفْسِ، وَعُقُوقُ الوَالِدَيْنِ. أَلَا أُنَبِّئُكُمْ بِأَكْبَرِ الكَبَائِرِ؟ قَوْلُ الزُّورِ.» أَوْ قَالَ: «شَهَادَةُ الزُّورِ.» [مُتَّفَقٌ عَلَيْهِ]

On the authority of Anas (may Allah be pleased with him): The Messenger of Allah (may Allah raise his rank and grant him peace) was asked about the major sins. He replied, **"Ascribing partners to Allah, murder, and disrespecting parents. Shall I not inform you of the greatest of the [other] major sins? False speech!"** Or he said, **"False testimony [as part of a conspiracy]!"** [Agreed upon]

24.6 BENEFITS OF THE HADEETH

Anas	
Asking about major sins	
Three major sins	1
	2
	3
Special focus on false speech	
Sunnah of repetition	

"He would not stop..."	
The obligation of honesty	

24.7 RESEARCH: Use the book, *al-Kabaa'ir* (the Major Sins), authored by Imaam ath-Thahabee (d.748), to summarize at least ten major sins and their evidences. Cite the number of the major sin according to the author's numbering (as done in the first example).

#	Major Sin	Evidence [and Comments]
6	Breaking fast in the daytime of Ramadhaan without an excuse	

THE LONG OVERDUE REVIVAL OF OUR HEARTS

25.1 QURAN STUDY

> أَلَمْ يَأْنِ لِلَّذِينَ ءَامَنُوٓاْ أَن تَخْشَعَ قُلُوبُهُمْ لِذِكْرِ ٱللَّهِ وَمَا نَزَلَ مِنَ ٱلْحَقِّ وَلَا
>
> يَكُونُواْ كَٱلَّذِينَ أُوتُواْ ٱلْكِتَٰبَ مِن قَبْلُ فَطَالَ عَلَيْهِمُ ٱلْأَمَدُ فَقَسَتْ قُلُوبُهُمْ وَكَثِيرٌ مِّنْهُمْ
>
> فَٰسِقُونَ ۞ الحديد: ١٦

"Has not the time come for the hearts of those who believe to render themselves in humility to the Remembrance of Allah and what has been revealed of the Truth? And that they not resemble those given the Book previously? The term became long to them, and their hearts hardened, while many of them were disobedient." [57:16]

25.2 VOCABULARY OF THE VERSE

لِذِكْرِ الله	أَنْ تَخْشَعَ قُلُوبُهُمْ	أَلَمْ يَأْنِ
فَطَالَ عَلَيْهِمُ الأَمَدُ	وَلَا يَكُونُوا	وَمَا نَزَلَ مِنَ الحَقّ
فَاسِقُونَ	وَكَثِيرٌ مِنْهُمْ	فَقَسَتْ قُلُوبُهُمْ

25.3 AN ARABIC LANGUAGE BENEFIT

TIP: *Review 8.3 about plural nouns.*

Plural nouns in the irregular "*takseer*" form, like قُلُوب, are commonly treated as feminine in grammar, even if the singular form is clearly masculine. Consider how this is found twice in the Verse, with both a past and present tense verbs changing to feminine versions when

105

connected to the plural noun, قلوب. Then consider the remaining examples and fill in the rest of the table, adding one more example that you find in your reading of Quran:

جمع	مفرد
﴿ أَن تَخْشَعَ قُلُوبُهُمْ ﴾	أَنْ يَخْشَعَ قَلْبُهُ
﴿ فَقَسَتْ قُلُوبُهُمْ ﴾	فَقَسَا قَلْبُهُ
﴿ وَأْتُوا الْبُيُوتَ مِنْ أَبْوَابِهَا ﴾ البقرة: ١٨٩	وَأْتُوا الْبَيْتَ مِنْ بَابِهِ
﴿ ﴾ القارعة: ٥	وَيَكُونُ الْجَبَلُ كَالْعِهْنِ الْمَنْفُوشِ
﴿ ﴾ القارعة: ٦	فَأَمَّا مَنْ ثَقُلَ مِيزَانُهُ
﴿ وَأَمَّا مَنْ خَفَّتْ مَوَازِينُهُ ﴾ القارعة: ٨	
﴿ ﴾	﴿ ﴾

25.4 TAFSEER BENEFITS

Has not the time come?	
Humility of the hearts	
The remembrance of Allah	
And what has been sent down	
Not resembling *Ahlul-Kitaab*	
Patience is of three types:	1
	2
	3
Time passing without reflection	
Hardness of the hearts	
Disobedience & the heart	

Abdullaah ibn Mas'ood said:	
Ibn 'Umar's night prayers	
The story of Fudhayl b. 'Eyaadh (not authentic)	

25.5 HADEETH STUDY

عَنْ أَبِي هُرَيْرَةَ رَضِيَ اللهُ عَنْهُ، قَالَ: قَالَ رَسُولُ اللهِ صَلَّى اللهُ عَلَيْهِ وَسَلَّمَ: «لَا تُكْثِرُوا الضَّحِكَ، فَإِنَّ كَثْرَةَ الضَّحِكِ تُمِيتُ الْقَلْبَ!» [أخرجه ابن ماجه، وصححه الألباني]

On the authority of Aboo Hurayrah (may Allah be pleased with him), the Messenger of Allah (may Allah raise his rank and grant him peace) said: **"Do not laugh too much, for excessive laughter does indeed kill the heart!"** [Ibn Maajah, authentic]

25.6 BENEFITS OF THE HADEETH

Aboo Hurayrah	
Excessive laughter	
Impermissible joking	1
	2
	3
Permissible joking within limits	
Hearts can actually die	
Behavior can kill the heart	
"If you knew what I know…"	1

	2
The modern "comedy" genre	
Culture that allows/encourages joking about everything	

25.7 RESEARCH AND CONTEMPLATION: List the violations of Islamic manners found in the comedy genre of today's entertainment and popular culture all around us.

RELIGIOUS LOYALTY AND ALLEGIANCE

26.1 QURAN STUDY

يَـٰٓأَيُّهَا ٱلَّذِينَ ءَامَنُوا لَا تَتَّخِذُوا عَدُوِّي وَعَدُوَّكُمْ أَوْلِيَاءَ تُلْقُونَ إِلَيْهِم بِٱلْمَوَدَّةِ وَقَدْ كَفَرُوا بِمَا جَاءَكُم مِّنَ ٱلْحَقِّ يُخْرِجُونَ ٱلرَّسُولَ وَإِيَّاكُمْ أَن تُؤْمِنُوا بِٱللَّهِ رَبِّكُمْ إِن كُنتُمْ خَرَجْتُمْ جِهَادًا فِي سَبِيلِي وَٱبْتِغَاءَ مَرْضَاتِي تُسِرُّونَ إِلَيْهِم بِٱلْمَوَدَّةِ وَأَنَا أَعْلَمُ بِمَا أَخْفَيْتُمْ وَمَا أَعْلَنتُمْ وَمَن يَفْعَلْهُ مِنكُمْ فَقَدْ ضَلَّ سَوَاءَ ٱلسَّبِيلِ ﴿ الممتحنة: ١

"O you who have believed! Do not take My enemies and your enemies as allies, showing them affection, while they have disbelieved in what has come to you of the Truth. And they drove out the Messenger and yourselves because you had believed in Allah, your Lord! [Do not take them as allies] if you have indeed come forth to struggle in My way, and seeking My Pleasure. You secretly show them affection, while I know all that you hide and all that you display openly. And whoever of you does that has surely strayed far from the straight path." [60:1]

26.2 VOCABULARY OF THE VERSE

أَوْلِيَاءَ	عَدُوِّي وَعَدُوَّكُم	لَا تَتَّخِذُوا
فِي سَبِيلِي	خَرَجْتُمْ جِهَادًا	تُلْقُونَ إِلَيْهِمْ بِالْمَوَدَّةِ
بِمَا أَخْفَيْتُمْ	تُسِرُّونَ إِلَيْهِمْ بِالْمَوَدَّةِ	وَابْتِغَاءَ مَرْضَاتِي
	ضَلَّ سَوَاءَ السَّبِيلِ	وَمَا أَعْلَنْتُمْ

26.3 AN ARABIC LANGUAGE BENEFIT

In any language, you can gauge your level of comprehension by checking how well you can connect the pronouns to the nouns they refer back to, their antecedents. Stop at the following pronouns found in our Verse and try to identify their antecedents, as done in the first few examples. Add two more pronouns from the Verse as well.

Antecedent	Pronoun	Verse
اللّٰه	عَدُوِّي	﴿لَا تَتَّخِذُوا عَدُوِّي﴾
الذين آمنوا	وَعَدُوَّكُم	﴿وَعَدُوَّكُمْ أَوْلِيَاءَ﴾
أعداء الله	إِلَيْهِم	﴿تُلْقُونَ إِلَيْهِم بِالْمَوَدَّةِ﴾
	جَاءَكُم	﴿وَقَدْ كَفَرُوا بِمَا جَاءَكُم مِّنَ ٱلْحَقِّ﴾
		﴿يُخْرِجُونَ ٱلرَّسُولَ وَإِيَّاكُم﴾
		﴿أَن تُؤْمِنُوا بِٱللَّهِ رَبِّكُم﴾
		﴿إِن كُنتُمْ خَرَجْتُمْ جِهَادًا فِي سَبِيلِي﴾
		﴿وَٱبْتِغَاءَ مَرْضَاتِي﴾

26.4 TAFSEER BENEFITS

The call: "O you who believe..."	
The prohibition	
"My and your" enemies	
The meaning of *"owliyaa"*	
Their opposition & animosity:	1

	2
Jihaad in the Way of Allah	
Seeking the Pleasure of Allah	
Secretly showing them affection	
Allah knows all (open & hidden)	
Taking them as allies is clear misguidance	
Non-Muslims without animosity	60:8
	60:9
Kindness vs. religious allegiance	

26.5 HADEETH STUDY

عَنْ أَبِي هُرَيْرَةَ رَضِيَ اللهُ عَنْهُ، عَنِ النَّبِيِّ صَلَّى اللهُ عَلَيْهِ وَسَلَّمَ، قَالَ: «الْمَرْءُ عَلَى دِينِ خَلِيلِهِ، فَلْيَنْظُرْ أَحَدُكُمْ مَنْ يُخَالِلُ.» [أَخْرَجَهُ أَحْمَدُ وَأَبُو دَاوُدَ وَالتِّرْمِذِيُّ، وَصَحَّحَهُ الْأَلْبَانِيُّ]

On the authority of Aboo Hurayrah (may Allah be pleased with him), from the Prophet (may Allah raise his rank and grant him peace), who said: "**A person is on the religion of his close friend, so let each of you look critically at the one he takes as a close friend.**" [Ahmad, Aboo Daawood, and at-Tirmithee, authentic]

111

26.6 BENEFITS OF THE HADEETH

Aboo Hurayrah	
What is a "*khaleel*"?	
Companionship is part of Islam	
The Salaf & companionship	1
	2
	3
The company of disbelievers	
The company of sinners	
The company of innovators	

26.7 PERSONAL PLANNING:
Think carefully about your current companions. Consider the best of them to be those who remind you about Allah, advise you, warn you from sins, encourage you towards obedience, and accompany you to prayers or Islamic classes, even if your time spent with them is very little. Consider the worst of them to be the ones who follow innovation and invite you to it, sin with you, or remain silent about your sins, flatter you, and those whose behavior leads you into worse behavior. Set up an action plan to take practical steps to take the time spent with the worst of them and give it to the best of them. **You will be upon the religion of your close companion. Remember to do this seeking the Pleasure of Allah alone.**

27.1 QURAN STUDY

۞ إِنَّ رَبَّكَ يَعْلَمُ أَنَّكَ تَقُومُ أَدْنَىٰ مِن ثُلُثَىِ ٱلَّيْلِ وَنِصْفَهُۥ وَثُلُثَهُۥ وَطَآئِفَةٌ مِّنَ ٱلَّذِينَ مَعَكَ وَٱللَّهُ يُقَدِّرُ ٱلَّيْلَ وَٱلنَّهَارَ عَلِمَ أَن لَّن تُحْصُوهُ فَتَابَ عَلَيْكُمْ فَٱقْرَءُوا۟ مَا تَيَسَّرَ مِنَ ٱلْقُرْءَانِ عَلِمَ أَن سَيَكُونُ مِنكُم مَّرْضَىٰ وَءَاخَرُونَ يَضْرِبُونَ فِى ٱلْأَرْضِ يَبْتَغُونَ مِن فَضْلِ ٱللَّهِ وَءَاخَرُونَ يُقَـٰتِلُونَ فِى سَبِيلِ ٱللَّهِ فَٱقْرَءُوا۟ مَا تَيَسَّرَ مِنْهُ وَأَقِيمُوا۟ ٱلصَّلَوٰةَ وَءَاتُوا۟ ٱلزَّكَوٰةَ وَأَقْرِضُوا۟ ٱللَّهَ قَرْضًا حَسَنًا وَمَا تُقَدِّمُوا۟ لِأَنفُسِكُم مِّنْ خَيْرٍ تَجِدُوهُ عِندَ ٱللَّهِ هُوَ خَيْرًا وَأَعْظَمَ أَجْرًا وَٱسْتَغْفِرُوا۟ ٱللَّهَ إِنَّ ٱللَّهَ غَفُورٌ رَّحِيمٌ ۞ المزمل: ٢٠

"Certainly your Lord knows that you stand (in prayer) less than two-thirds of the night, half of it, or a third of it, with a group of those with you. Allah determines both the night and the day. He knew that you would not precisely measure it (the time of the night), so He accepted your repentance. So then read whatever of the Quran is easy. He knew that some of you would be ill, others traveling about in the land seeking the bounties of Allah, and others fighting in the Way of Allah. So read whatever of it is easy, establish the prayer, pay *zakaat*, and lend unto Allah a goodly loan. And whatever amount of good you put forth for yourselves is better and greater for reward. And seek Allah's Forgiveness. Indeed Allah is All-Forgiving, Ever Merciful." [73:20]

27.2 VOCABULARY OF THE VERSE

وَنِصْفَهُ	ثُلُثَي اللَّيْلِ	أَدْنَى مِنْ
يُقَدِّرُ اللَّيْلَ وَالنَّهَارَ	وَطَائِفَةٌ	وَثُلُثَهُ
فَاقْرَؤُوا	فَتَابَ عَلَيْكُمْ	لَنْ تُحْصُوهُ
يَضْرِبُونَ فِي الْأَرْضِ	مَرْضَى	مَا تَيَسَّرَ
قَرْضًا حَسَنًا	وَأَقْرِضُوا اللهَ	يُقَاتِلُونَ فِي سَبِيلِ اللهِ

27.3 AN ARABIC LANGUAGE BENEFIT

Allah mentions a number of fractions in the Quran on the topics of night prayers, inheritance and distribution of the spoils of war, as summarized in the following table.

﴿ وَنِصْفَهُ ﴾	half	النِّصْفُ
﴿ وَثُلُثَهُ ﴾	one-third	الثُّلُثُ
﴿ وَلَهُنَّ الرُّبُعُ مِمَّا تَرَكْتُمْ ﴾ النساء: ١٢	one-fourth	الرُّبُعُ
﴿ فَأَنَّ لِلَّهِ خُمُسَهُ ﴾ الأنفال: ٤١	one-fifth	الخُمُسُ
﴿ وَلِأَبَوَيْهِ لِكُلِّ وَاحِدٍ مِنْهُمَا السُّدُسُ ﴾ النساء: ١١	one-sixth	السُّدُسُ
﴿ فَلَهُنَّ الثُّمُنُ مِمَّا تَرَكْتُمْ ﴾ النساء: ١٢	one-eighth	الثُّمُنُ

27.4 TAFSEER BENEFITS

The order for night prayers	
Allah knows our practice	
Allah's *taqdeer* of day & night	
Man's weakness	
Measuring the night is difficult	
Measuring the day is easier	
Repentance	
With hardships comes ease	
Night prayer is difficult for:	1
	2
	3
Rulings: case by case basis	
Healthy, safe residents	
The five directives	1
	2
	3
	4
	5
Lending unto Allah?	
Multiplied rewards for charity	
Orders given to the Prophet	

27.5 HADEETH STUDY

سُئِلَتْ عَائِشَةُ رَضِيَ اللهُ عَنْهَا: كَيْفَ كَانَتْ صَلَاةُ رَسُولِ اللهِ صَلَّى اللهُ عَلَيْهِ وَسَلَّمَ فِي رَمَضَانَ؟ فَقَالَتْ: مَا كَانَ رَسُولُ اللهِ صَلَّى اللهُ عَلَيْهِ وَسَلَّمَ يَزِيدُ فِي رَمَضَانَ وَلَا فِي غَيْرِهِ عَلَى إِحْدَى عَشْرَةَ رَكْعَةً، يُصَلِّي أَرْبَعًا، فَلَا تَسْأَلْ عَنْ حُسْنِهِنَّ وَطُولِهِنَّ! ثُمَّ يُصَلِّي أَرْبَعًا، فَلَا تَسْأَلْ عَنْ حُسْنِهِنَّ وَطُولِهِنَّ! ثُمَّ يُصَلِّي ثَلَاثًا. [مُتَّفَقٌ عَلَيْهِ]

'Aa'ishah (may Allah be pleased with her) was asked about the [night] prayer of the Messenger of Allah (may Allah raise his rank and grant him peace). She said: He did not used to pray more than 11 *rak'ahs* in Ramadhaan or outside of Ramadhaan. He would pray four, and do not even ask about how fine and lengthy they were! Then he would pray four more, and do not even ask about how fine and lengthy they were! Then he would pray three. [Agreed upon]

27.6 BENEFITS OF THE HADEETH

'Aa'ishah	
The concern of this era	
Night prayers are for all year	
This description of prayer	

27.7 PERSONAL PLANNING: Some people in the West have very busy days. Based on what we have learned about the flexibility of night prayers, their virtues, and the importance of continuing to offer them throughout the year, develop a general plan for your night prayers, one that takes into considerations your personal difficulties throughout the week. Try to pray at least three *rak'ahs* when you are most busy, and plan to pray more on your weekends or the nights when you have more time in your schedule. **Do not be pleased with yourself only offering night prayers in Ramadhaan. Build on the good Allah has blessed you to establish this month.**

28.1 QURAN STUDY

وَالشَّمْسِ وَضُحَاهَا ۝ وَالْقَمَرِ إِذَا تَلَاهَا ۝ وَالنَّهَارِ إِذَا جَلَّاهَا ۝ وَاللَّيْلِ إِذَا يَغْشَاهَا ۝ وَالسَّمَاءِ وَمَا بَنَاهَا ۝ وَالْأَرْضِ وَمَا طَحَاهَا ۝ وَنَفْسٍ وَمَا سَوَّاهَا ۝ فَأَلْهَمَهَا فُجُورَهَا وَتَقْوَاهَا ۝ قَدْ أَفْلَحَ مَن زَكَّاهَا ۝ وَقَدْ خَابَ مَن دَسَّاهَا ۝ الشمس

"By the Sun and its early morning light. And by the Moon as it follows it (the Sun). And by the day as it openly features it. And by the night as it covers it up. And by the sky and how He built it. And by the earth and how He spread it out. And by a soul and how He proportioned it (perfectly), and then He led it to understand its evil and its piety. Certainly, successful is he who purifies it. And ruined is he who corrupts it (with sin)." [91:1-10]

28.2 VOCABULARY OF THE VERSE

وَالْقَمَرِ إِذَا تَلَاهَا	وَضُحَاهَا	وَالشَّمْسِ
والسَّمَاءِ	وَاللَّيْلِ إِذَا يَغْشَاهَا	وَالنَّهَارِ إِذَا جَلَّاهَا
وَمَا طَحَاهَا	وَالْأَرْضِ	وَمَا بَنَاهَا
فَأَلْهَمَهَا فُجُورَهَا	وَمَا سَوَّاهَا	وَنَفْسٍ
وَقَدْ خَابَ مَن دَسَّاهَا	قَدْ أَفْلَحَ مَن زَكَّاهَا	وَتَقْوَاهَا

28.3 AN ARABIC LANGUAGE BENEFIT

One of the uses of the letter "waaw" in the Arabic Language is to swear by something. This is done by putting what is called a "waaw al-qasam" in front of a noun and changing the case of that noun to *majroor*. This has been done many times in the Verse we have studied, as summarized in the table below. Add some Verses from the 30th part of the Quran which also include *waaw al-qasam*.

﴿ وَٱلنَّهَارِ ﴾	﴿ وَٱلۡقَمَرِ ﴾	﴿ وَٱلشَّمۡسِ ﴾
﴿ وَٱلۡأَرۡضِ ﴾	﴿ وَٱلسَّمَآءِ ﴾	﴿ وَٱلَّيۡلِ ﴾
		﴿ وَٱلتِّينِ وَٱلزَّيۡتُونِ ﴾

Remember: Swearing by other than Allah is not allowed for us, while Allah may swear by whatever of His Creation He so chooses.

28.4 TAFSEER BENEFITS

Things sworn by	
	1
	2
	3
	4
	5
	6
	7
	8
	9
	10
	11

"Jawaab al-Qasam"	
Purification of the soul	
Corruption of the soul	

28.5 HADEETH STUDY

عَنْ زَيْدِ بْنِ أَرْقَمَ رَضِيَ اللهُ عَنْهُ: أَنَّ رَسُولَ اللهِ صَلَّى اللهُ عَلَيْهِ وَسَلَّمَ كَانَ يَقُولُ: «اللَّهُمَّ إِنِّي أَعُوذُ بِكَ مِنَ العَجْزِ، وَالكَسَلِ، وَالجُبْنِ، وَالبُخْلِ، وَالهَرَمِ، وَعَذَابِ القَبْرِ. اللَّهُمَّ آتِ نَفْسِي تَقْوَاهَا، وَزَكِّهَا أَنْتَ خَيْرُ مَنْ زَكَّاهَا، أَنْتَ وَلِيُّهَا وَمَوْلَاهَا. اللَّهُمَّ إِنِّي أَعُوذُ بِكَ مِنْ عِلْمٍ لَا يَنْفَعُ، وَمِنْ قَلْبٍ لَا يَخْشَعُ، وَمِنْ نَفْسٍ لَا تَشْبَعُ، وَمِنْ دَعْوَةٍ لَا يُسْتَجَابُ لَهَا» [أَخْرَجَهُ مُسْلِمٌ]

On the authority of Zayd ibn Arqam (may Allah be pleased with him), who said: The Messenger of Allah (may Allah raise his rank and grant him peace) used to supplicate: **"O Allah, I do seek refuge with You from incapability, laziness, cowardice, stinginess, senility, and the torment of the grave. O Allah, give my soul its piety and purify it. You are the best to purify it; You are its guardian and caretaker. O Allah, I do seek refuge with You from knowledge without benefit, a heart that has no humility, a soul that does not attain contentment, and a supplication that gets no response."** [*Saheeh Muslim*]

28.6 BENEFITS OF THE HADEETH

Zayd ibn Arqam	
Seeking refuge (as worship)	
Serious flaws in character	1

	2	
	3	
	4	
	5	
The punishment of the grave		
Asking Allah to purify one's soul		
Four disastrous situations	1	
	2	
	3	
	4	

28.7 MEMORIZATION: Learn and memorize the supplication from 28.5 to use often. It can be easier to memorize if you break it up into three parts, as done for you below:

اللّهُمَّ إِنِّي أَعُوذُ بِكَ مِنَ الْعَجْزِ، وَالْكَسَلِ، وَالْجُبْنِ،
وَالْبُخْلِ، وَالْهَرَمِ، وَعَذَابِ الْقَبْرِ.

اللّهُمَّ آتِ نَفْسِي تَقْوَاهَا، وَزَكِّهَا، أَنْتَ خَيْرُ مَنْ زَكَّاهَا،
أَنْتَ وَلِيُّهَا وَمَوْلَاهَا.

اللّهُمَّ إِنِّي أَعُوذُ بِكَ مِنْ عِلْمٍ لَا يَنْفَعُ، وَمِنْ قَلْبٍ لَا يَخْشَعُ،
وَمِنْ نَفْسٍ لَا تَشْبَعُ، وَمِنْ دَعْوَةٍ لَا يُسْتَجَابُ لَهَا

29.1 QURAN STUDY

> ﴿ إِنَّا أَعْطَيْنَاكَ ٱلْكَوْثَرَ ﴿١﴾ فَصَلِّ لِرَبِّكَ وَٱنْحَرْ ﴿٢﴾ إِنَّ شَانِئَكَ هُوَ ٱلْأَبْتَرُ ﴿٣﴾ ﴾ الكوثر

"Verily, We have given you the *Kowthar*. So pray to your Lord and slaughter. Your abusive opponent is indeed cut off. [108:1-3]

29.2 VOCABULARY OF THE VERSE

إِنَّ شَانِئَكَ هُوَ الْأَبْتَرُ	فَصَلِّ لِرَبِّكَ وَانْحَرْ	إِنَّا أَعْطَيْنَاكَ الْكَوْثَرَ

29.3 AN ARABIC LANGUAGE BENEFIT

The verb, أعطى, like our English verb, **to give**, is a special transitive verb, having two objects. You give someone something. Consider the following breakdown of the two objects, and try to complete the table:

الْمَفْعُولُ الثَّانِي	الْمَفْعُولُ الْأَوَّلُ	الْمِثَالُ
الْكَوْثَرَ	أَنْتَ (مُحَمَّدًا)	﴿ إِنَّا أَعْطَيْنَاكَ ٱلْكَوْثَرَ ﴾
دِينَارًا	خَالِدًا	أَعْطَى مُحَمَّدٌ خَالِدًا دِينَارًا
دِرْهَمًا	هُ (هُوَ)	أَعْطَاهُ زَيْدٌ دِرْهَمًا
هَا (هِيَ)	نِي (أَنَا)	أَعْطَانِيهَا

121

		أَعْطَى الرَّجُلُ ابْنَهُ الْمِفْتَاح
		أَعْطَتْهُ زَوْجَتُهُ هَدِيَّةً
		أَعْطَاهُمْ رَبُّهُمْ جَزَاءً حَسَنًا

29.4 TAFSEER BENEFITS

The shortest *soorah*	
A reminder of a blessing	
What is the "*Kowthar*"?	1
	2
	3
	4
The order for prayer	
The order for *nahr* (slaughter)	
These two actions together	6:162-163
Your opponent	
The meaning of being cut off	

29.5 HADEETH STUDY

عَنْ أَنَسٍ رَضِيَ اللهُ عَنْهُ، قَالَ: قَالَ رَسُولُ اللهِ صَلَّى اللهُ عَلَيْهِ وَسَلَّمَ: «أَتَدْرُونَ مَا الْكَوْثَرُ؟» فَقُلْنَا: اللهُ وَرَسُولُهُ أَعْلَمُ. قَالَ: «فَإِنَّهُ نَهْرٌ وَعَدَنِيهِ رَبِّي عَزَّ وَجَلَّ، عَلَيْهِ خَيْرٌ كَثِيرٌ، هُوَ حَوْضٌ تَرِدُ عَلَيْهِ أُمَّتِي يَوْمَ الْقِيَامَةِ، آنِيَتُهُ عَدَدُ النُّجُومِ، فَيُخْتَلَجُ الْعَبْدُ مِنْهُمْ، فَأَقُولُ: رَبِّ! إِنَّهُ مِنْ أُمَّتِي! فَيَقُولُ: مَا تَدْرِي مَا أَحْدَثَ بَعْدَكَ!» [أَخْرَجَهُ مُسْلِمٌ]

On the authority of Anas (may Allah be pleased with him): The Messenger of Allah (may Allah raise his rank and grant him peace) said: **"Do you know what the** *Kowthar* **is?"** We said, "Allah and His Messenger know best." He said, **"It is a river which my Lord, the Mighty and Majestic, has promised me. Upon it is abundant good, a pool which my nation shall gather at to drink from on the Day of Resurrection. Its drinking vessels are the number of the stars. A worshipper will be blocked off from it, and I shall say: 'My Lord! He is one of my followers!' And He will say: 'You do not know what he did after you!'"** [*Saheeh Muslim*]

29.6 BENEFITS OF THE HADEETH

Anas	
"*Hadeeth qudsee*" (partially)	
The teacher asks a question	
Students respond, engage	
Saying "Allah knows best"	
The *Kowthar* is a river	

Shown and promised	
It is connected to the *howdh*	
His followers drink from it	
Numerous drinking vessels	
His concern for all followers	
He does not know the *ghayb*	
Innovation leads to deprival	

29.7 REMINDER: Be sure that you have either distributed your *Zakaat al-Fitr* by now, or you have prepared it for distribution. Offer your assistance to those who may need help in doing so. Review Lesson 21 about *Zakaat al-Fitr* if needed.

30.1 QURAN STUDY

قُلْ هُوَ ٱللَّهُ أَحَدٌ ۝ ٱللَّهُ ٱلصَّمَدُ ۝ لَمْ يَلِدْ وَلَمْ يُولَدْ ۝ وَلَمْ يَكُن لَّهُ كُفُوًا أَحَدٌ ۝ الإخلاص

"Say: He is Allah, Uniquely One. Allah, the One Whom all rely upon. He did not beget [offspring], nor was He begotten. And there is none comparable to Him." [112:1-4]

30.2 VOCABULARY OF THE VERSE

اللهُ الصَّمَدُ	أَحَدٌ	قُلْ هُوَ اللهُ
وَلَمْ يَكُنْ لَهُ كُفُوًا أَحَدٌ	وَلَمْ يُولَدْ	لَمْ يَلِدْ

30.3 AN ARABIC LANGUAGE BENEFIT

The word لم is used to negate a present tense verb. It causes the verb to change cases, to become *majzoom*. There are three examples of this in the Soorah, as listed in the following table. Try to complete the table as needed.

لَمْ + المُضَارِع	الفِعْلُ
﴿لَمْ يَلِدْ﴾	وَلَدَ يَلِدُ
﴿وَلَمْ يُولَدْ﴾	أُولِدَ يُولَدُ

كَانَ يَكُونُ	﴿ ﴾	﴿ لَّهُۥ كُفُوًا أَحَدُۢ ﴾
عَلِمَ يَعْلَمُ	﴿ عَلَّمَ ٱلْإِنسَٰنَ ﴾ العلق: ٥	
	﴿ أَيَحْسَبُ أَن لَّمْ يَرَهُۥٓ أَحَدُ ﴾ البلد: ٧	
	﴿ ﴾ الفجر: ٨	

30.4 TAFSEER BENEFITS

The *"sabab an-nuzool"*	
Some virtues of this *soorah*	1
	2
Proclaiming Allah's Oneness	
The meaning of *"as-Samad"*	
Negation of parent/child	
Negation of *"tash-beeh"*	
Understanding Divine Attributes	
Deviations in this topic:	1
	2
	3
	4
	5

30.5 HADEETH STUDY

عَنْ أَبِي هُرَيْرَةَ رَضِيَ اللهُ عَنْهُ، قَالَ: قَالَ رَسُولُ اللهِ صَلَّى اللهُ عَلَيْهِ وَسَلَّمَ: «قَالَ اللهُ: كَذَّبَنِي ابْنُ آدَمَ وَلَمْ يَكُنْ لَهُ ذَلِكَ، وَشَتَمَنِي وَلَمْ يَكُنْ لَهُ ذَلِكَ. فَأَمَّا تَكْذِيبُهُ إِيَّايَ، فَقَوْلُهُ "لَنْ يُعِيدَنِي كَمَا بَدَأَنِي"، وَلَيْسَ أَوَّلُ الْخَلْقِ بِأَهْوَنَ عَلَيَّ مِنْ إِعَادَتِهِ. وَأَمَّا شَتْمُهُ إِيَّايَ، فَقَوْلُهُ "اتَّخَذَ اللهُ وَلَدًا"، وَأَنَا الْأَحَدُ الصَّمَدُ، لَمْ أَلِدْ وَلَمْ أُولَدْ، وَلَمْ يَكُنْ لِي كُفُوًا أَحَدٌ!» [أخرجه البخاري]

On the authority of Aboo Hurayrah (may Allah be pleased with him) who said: The Messenger of Allah (may Allah raise his rank and grant him peace) said: "Allah has said: The son of Adam belies Me, with no grounds to do so; He insults Me, with no grounds to do so. As for his belying of Me, then it is his claim, 'He shall not resurrect me as I was created before.' Yet, the initial creating of everything was no easier to Me than bringing it back. As for his insulting of Me, then it is his claim, 'Allah has taken a son,' whilst I am the Singular One, the Divinely Self-Sufficient One, I did not beget (anyone), nor was I begotten, and there is none comparable to Me!" [Saheeh al-Bukhaaree]

30.6 BENEFITS OF THE HADEETH

Aboo Hurayrah	
Hadeeth qudsee	
Generalizing the majority	
Blasphemous verbal offenses	1
	2
Denying resurrection is disbelief	

The polytheism of Christians	
Allah's Names in this hadeeth	1
	2

30.7 RESEARCH: Find the following Names of Allah in the Quran, and then add more to the table, as many as you are able.

Verse	Meaning	Transliterated	Name
1:2	The All-Merciful	Ar-Rahmaan	﴿ ٱلرَّحۡمَٰنِ ﴾
1:2	The Ever Merciful	Ar-Raheem	﴿ ٱلرَّحِيمِ ﴾
		Al-A'laa	﴿ ٱلۡأَعۡلَىٰ ﴾
85:8			﴿ ٱلۡعَزِيزِ ﴾
85:8			﴿ ٱلۡحَمِيدِ ﴾
			﴿ ٱلۡغَفُورُ ﴾
			﴿ ٱلۡوَدُودُ ﴾

AL-HAMDU LILLAAH

This completes our study of these thirty Quranic passages, and all praise is due to Allah, the only One who facilitates success.

رَّبَّنَا إِنَّنَا سَمِعْنَا مُنَادِيًا يُنَادِي لِلْإِيمَٰنِ أَنْ ءَامِنُوا۟ بِرَبِّكُمْ فَـَٔامَنَّا

رَبَّنَا فَٱغْفِرْ لَنَا ذُنُوبَنَا وَكَفِّرْ عَنَّا سَيِّـَٔاتِنَا

وَتَوَفَّنَا مَعَ ٱلْأَبْرَارِ

آل عمران
١٩٣

Our Lord! We have heard a caller calling to eemaan,
saying: 'Believe in your Lord!' So we have believed.

Our Lord! Forgive us for our sins,
and expiate from us our bad deeds.

And take our souls along with the righteous.

[3:193]

If you liked these lessons, then study two more courses, using the free recordings available from the 2018 Summer Courses at TROID, along with the workbook from Amazon.com:

Made in the USA
Middletown, DE
20 May 2021